STATE vs. CHURCH

WHAT CHRISTIANS CAN DO TO SAVE CANADA FROM LIBERAL TYRANNY

TIMOTHY BLOEDOW

Published by
Bloedow, Timothy
Printed in the United States of America

ISBN 978-0-9782942-1-2

First Edition

TABLE OF CONTENTS

AKNOWLEDGEMENTS

There are many individuals whom I should like to thank for making this book possible. First and foremost, I should like to thank my wife, Lynette, who says that she has seen these ideas percolating for 15 years. I don't think I can see further back than 5 years. Through many circumstances over the years, she has supported and encouraged my passion for writing through many different avenues. On our wedding day, my song to her was "You are the Wind Beneath My Wings." That holds true now more than ever—although I have no idea where she gets her stamina to keep me going.

I should also like to thank my father, who has supported my writing endeavours. This is an area where I take after him, although in a rather different field, he being a specialist in Classics, Ancient History and Archaeology. I should also like to pay tribute to my late mother, a scholar, scientist and very avid reader. She showed great interest in everything I wrote, and supported all my efforts, from the very beginning. I am very appreciative of my father's work in editing my manuscript. I should also like to express my gratitude to the others who also kindly edited and examined my manuscript from several different angles to improve the final product. They include

Christian Heritage Party leader Ron Gray, journalist Rory Leishman, Grace Presbyterian Church (Associate Reformed Synod) minister Rev. Jeff Kingswood, Family Coalition Party of Ontario leader Giuseppe Gori, journalist Tony Gosnach, Citizens Centre for Freedom and Democracy chairman Link Byfield and friend and colleague Mark Penninga.

I should also like to thank Compass Creative for the excellent quality of their work designing the cover of this book and designing the website which complements the book at www.christiangovernment.ca.

There are many others who have also provided necessary guidance and encouragement in the process, which has led to the publication of the book you are holding today. I say, "thank you," to each of you.

"Where there is no vision the people perish."

This passage from Proverbs 29:18 in the Holy Bible is found carved in stone, framing a window on the West side of the Peace Tower.

PREFACE

Some Christians hold the view that the civil magistrate—commonly called the government—is a necessary evil. Other Christians hold the position that the civil government is an institution established by God, one of four governmental orders given to us by God to establish a just and viable civil-social order for living in this world. (The three other governments ordained by God are church government, family government and self-government.) We hold to the latter position.

This book is a challenge to readers as to the way that Christians should think about civil politics, but not civil politics standing alone. One of the biggest controversies in Canada today is over the correct relationship between the state and the Church. Clarifying the Christian position on this issue is the heart of this book. In discussing the relationship between the Church and the state, we also examine the relationship between religion and (civil) politics, the relationship between religion and the state and, to a lesser degree, the relationship between the state and the family, and the relationship between the state and the individual.

In this book, we shall affirm some beliefs already widely held by Christians regarding this broad topic of Church/state relations. We shall also expose many myths, some advanced by our Secular Humanist opponents; others accepted by Christians. In some cases, we challenge Christians to reject more explicitly the unchristian paradigms by which Secular Humanists have framed the current controversy. For example, we expose and rebut the assumption that (Christian) religion is at odds with science and reason. We also challenge the notion that Secular Humanism is morally neutral and demonstrate that Secular Humanism is religious in nature.

Without understanding these assumptions, it will be impossible for Christians to win the culture war that is raging in Canada. Secular Humanists argue that the options before us are a civil government that is influenced by religion or a Secular Humanist civil government that is morally neutral and pluralistic, a philosophical zone into which people from all different views can meet to establish common public policy. This is one of the most dangerous—and fundamentally false—views held by Canada's establishment leaders today, but it is also unfortunately one of the most widely held ideas throughout our country.

We also demonstrate that Christianity is the philosophical (and theological) source of the principle of equality before the law, the rule of law, real justice, individual liberty and a functioning order for social peace. Secular Humanism claims all these things but is, in fact, the source of growing anarchy and tyranny. Secularism is advancing the socialistic concepts of group rights and equality of outcome, special rights and competing interests, pandering politics and the idolatry of a centralized civil government that rules over all of life. This all-pervasive idea of civil government as god has today's government even claiming the authority and right to redefine the natural order so as to sanction "same-sex marriage" and the right of people to assert a gender irrespective of the bodily organs with which they were conceived.

Christians have nothing to be ashamed of when they assert the Lordship of Christ over the civil government, when they propose distinctly Christian laws, whether those laws ban murder and theft or whether they define marriage as between one man and one woman.

We expose the myths by which Secular Humanists denigrate Christianity and the contribution of Christians to public policy and civil government. And we give Christians the intellectual tools they need to stand tall as they advance the claims of Christ in the public square, and as they offer explicitly Christian ideas for public policy for the Canada of the 21st century.[1]

---

[1] Let me note from the outset that this book includes a fair bit of polemic and strong language. This puts off some people. Some think that it is strategically unhelpful to use strong language. Some Christians simply see it as unchristian. Unfortunately, however, history is full of examples of corruption and harm continuing under the cover of polite and "sophisticated" debate. Sometimes it is necessary to be blunt and frank when identifying the true nature of corruption, especially when (some of) its victims are vulnerable and defenceless people. Whether you agree with the use of the strong language in this book, I wanted to make it clear from the start that where it is used, it is used intentionally and the language used is believed to be accurate. It is not simply knee-jerk invective. Neither is it *ad hominem*. I don't use harsh language as an argument. Nor does following Jesus' example in using strong language against His enemies, negate my commitment to His commandment to "love your enemies, bless them that curse you, do good to them that hate you, and pray for them which despitefully use you, and persecute you." Some of you may be aware that influential Secular Humanists use harsh language against Christians. The title of a new book written against American Christians is called, "American Fascists: The Christian Right and the War on America." I am not playing tit-for-tat, but neither am I responsible for raising the volume of this culture war between Christianity and Secular Humanism. It should also be noted that my argumentation gives the impression that I assume malicious intent on the part of Secular Humanists (a.k.a. modern liberals). It is not that I assume malicious intent on the part of all liberals, rather, my argumentation should be understood as assuming malicious intent on the part of many of those who are influential and many of those whom the mainstream media like to draw on as spokesmen for Secularism. I believe that the many examples in this book clearly demonstrate this malicious intent. You be the judge.

INTRODUCTION

The separation of church and state is a glorious Christian doctrine. It is not simply Christian culturally, as though it was simply co-opted and perfected by societies that happened to be significantly Christian. The separation of church and state is a biblical doctrine given to us by God as a gracious provision for the orderly functioning of society. It is an essential component of ordered liberty, the socio-political model given to us by God, and the Christian corrective to the non-Christian tendencies toward anarchy and tyranny. This ethic is one of accountability, decentralized governance, localism, individual liberty and self-government. This principle flows out of the recognition that God ordered this world covenantally[1] and created three covenantal institutions (the family, the church and the state), each with its own jurisdiction or sphere of governmental authority.

History provides us with regrettable examples of Christians who have pursued non-Christian approaches to society and

---

1. Among other things, this means that God has established a hierarchy to enforce His authority on earth, that He is the sovereign authority over that hierarchy and the governmental institutions he has established to enforce it, that His law is to guide the structure and operation of these institutions, and that God will judge man by how well he follows these rules.

governance in place of this glorious and gracious doctrine, as well as Christians who have joined others in the pursuit of worldly power instead of approaching political governance as a place of service. The Church has done much harm to itself and its witness in this world by ignoring this principle of separation of church and state and the broader ethic out of which it flows.

Even though the Church had problems in the past when it rejected the principle of the separation of church and state, Christians are rejecting it again today, but they are doing so because they aren't clear about the nature of the issue and because they have accepted the non-Christian redefinition of the term. What is this non-Christian redefinition? What has Canada's Secular Humanist establishment done to the term "separation of church and state" after it expropriated the language from Christianity? They have redefined it in such a way as to make the separation of church and state synonymous with the separation of religion—or at least the Christian religion—from politics. That is, they found a catch phrase to give them a plausible excuse to isolate politics from the influence of Christians.

Because theologically literate Christians understand that politics—or, more accurately, civil governance—should not be devoid of the influence of the Christian religion (i.e. they recognize the importance of "mixing" religion and politics), many of them are saying that they reject a belief in the separation of church and state. This, however, is not a helpful position for Christians to take. Christians need to argue vigorously for the separation of the institutional roles of the church and the state—while, simultaneously, and just as vigorously, contending for the influence of Christianity in the civil governance of Canada. More than that, as we shall see,

Christians should be arguing for the centrality of Christian principles—and through them, the Lordship of the gracious God of creation and redemption—over the civil governance of this nation. We need to re-educate ourselves about the morally superior nature of Christianity for law and public policy, as well as for private morality, identifying the ways in which Christianity applies the grace of God in society.

Of the various expressions of religion that compete with Christianity for the hearts and minds of Canadians, the dominant one today is the ideology of Secular Humanism. Secular Humanism and liberalism can be treated as almost synonymous concepts today. Secularism, therefore, is the focus of our analysis in this book when it comes to discussing the current controversy over the separation of church and state, and the culture war that is taking place in Canada. It is time to understand this controversy clearly, to stake out a clear Christian position, and to use this Christian position to take back confidently and relentlessly the ground stolen by Secular Humanists in their campaign to become the driving force and establishment voice in Canada.

We shall demonstrate that the real battle over the separation of church and state is to confine the state in the limited sphere given it by God. To do this, individuals need to renew their commitment to self-government, the foundation of noble character, and the kind of personal responsibility that is essential to sustaining civilization. Families and churches also need to rediscover the governmental components of their divine mandates, reclaiming the jurisdictions of life over which they should govern, but which the state currently controls.

We shall begin with a discussion of several examples of what the "separation of church and state" does not mean (Chapters 1-3). This will be followed by an explanation of what the term does mean (Chapter 4). The fifth chapter will provide a thorough discussion of the way in which the state has overstepped the legitimate parameters of its jurisdiction. It addresses the implications of this socialist trend for the replacement of individual liberty and genuine equality with tyranny, a process that is already well underway in Canada. The final chapter explores some key details in terms of how Christian-based civil governance differs from Secular Humanist social theory, with a special emphasis on the contrast between the liberty principle of Christianity and the oppressive tyranny of Secularism.

This book will be successful if you walk away from it with a better understanding of the Christian worldview, and knowing that it includes a political theory, that liberty is foundational to this political theory, that it is antithetical to Secular Humanism (the leading alternative fighting for political dominance in Canada), that it is morally and intellectually superior to Secularism and all other contenders. But more than that, upon finishing this book, you hopefully will be convinced that Christians have not simply a right, but an obligation before God, to advance the propositions for their worldview in Canada's public square with the goal of seeing them adopted and Canada once again reformed by way of a comprehensive return to Christian faith, including in terms of civil governance and public policy, not simply because we think they are right, but because we know they offer all Canadians the most gracious, charitable, productive, restorative model for social order.

CHAPTER ONE

SEPARATION OF CHURCH AND STATE;
NOT THE SEPARATION OF RELIGION FROM POLITICS

Christians have become increasingly uncomfortable in recent years with the terminology of "separation of church and state" because Secular Humanists have achieved a measure of success using that terminology against them. Secular Humanism is the religion or ideology that drives Canada's current liberal Establishment. Secular Humanism is driving Canada's cultural reformation today and is contending most vigorously for ideological control over Canada's power structures. The most important battle in today's culture wars is between Christianity and this Secular Humanism, hence the focus of this book as we look at what Christians need to do to re-assert the cultural leadership they once held in Canada.

Instead of giving in to the Secularists who have re-defined the language of "separation of church and state" to also argue against the influence of Christian religion on politics,

Christians need to take back the language, define it correctly and use it as part of their arsenal in the ongoing culture war against Secular Humanism. The separation of church and state is an essential Christian doctrine—when it is understood and applied correctly. The idea of separation of church and state—that the institutions of the church and the state have distinct roles to play in society—as applied following the Protestant Reformation, was foundational to the development of democratic principles: ordered liberty and equality before the law. This was evident in the establishment of the form of government known as a constitutional monarchy within the British Empire, as well as the republican experiment in the United States.

The need for a division of authority was recognized as necessary within the state itself, but there was also the belief that the state shared authority in society with the church—and with families and individuals by virtue of the recognition of a broad realm of private life that did not require regulation and micro-management by the state. It is out of this concept of organizational and governmental decentralization that a correct understanding of the term "separation of church and state" flows. Another term used for this concept, at least within Reformed Christian circles, is "sphere sovereignty."[1]

As was noted in the Introduction of this book, Secularists have co-opted the term "separation of church and state," redefining it also to mean the separation of religion from politics. As a result, Liberal MP Pierre Pettigrew (Papineau, QC), greatly embarrassed himself (not that he realized this to be the case) in

1. Within Catholic theology, a similar concept is used: the principle of "subsidiarity," according to which the levels of government of a larger and more distant nature (local, regional, provincial and national) are subsidiary, and not superior, to the forms of government closer to the individual (individual self-government and family government). This principle essentially states that what can be done by the individual, the family, church groups or local associations—or by more local levels of government—should not be performed by a distant bureaucracy.

the midst of the marriage definition controversy in Canada in early 2005. Mr. Pettigrew, a Liberal Cabinet Minister (Minister of Foreign Affairs) at the time, and ostensibly a Roman Catholic, but in reality a Secularist, condemned the public comments by Catholic clergy against the government's plans to redefine marriage. Thinking he was marshalling a good Secularist argument against obnoxious, interfering religious leaders, he said: "I find that the separation of the church and the state is one of the most beautiful inventions of modern times."[2]

Yes the separation of church and state is a beautiful idea, Mr. Pettigrew. But not for the reasons you suppose—and it is not an invention of modern times. In fact you are calling to your defence a profoundly religious—Christian—argument that, rightly understood, has nothing to do with what you are really trying to say.

Christians marginalize themselves when they allow intellectually inferior and morally debased Secular Humanism to dictate the terms of debate in Canada's culture war. Instead of accepting their opponents' framing of the argument, Christians need to mount a strong defence for the importance of the separation of church and state while simultaneously fighting for the primary role that Christianity should play in civil governance and the development of public policy in Canada. This stance is not simply important for asserting the rightful role of Christianity in Canada's public square, but also, as we shall soon see, for providing the rationale for a radical roll-back of the state to its legitimate sphere of governance. Consistent with the radical socialist ideology that Secular Humanism represents, the Canadian state in recent

2. "Church told to butt out: Same-sex debate no place for religion: Pettigrew," by Elizabeth Thompson and Anne Dawson. *National Post*, January 28, 2005.

years has interposed itself substantially into the spheres of jurisdiction that rightfully belong to the family, the church and individual privacy.

The battle over the term "separation of church and state" and its meaning is essential because the phrase has almost taken on a life of its own, as it has become a cult-like mantra exploited for its emotional impact by anti-intellectual Secularists who want to ban every public expression of Christian faith. The following is a typical example of this militant agenda. When someone uses the term "separation of church and state," one would expect him to be dealing with an issue that pertains to the church and to the state. We learn from the following example, however, that this is not necessarily the case. In commenting in October 2005 on a case of a lesbian suing Christian doctors who would not artificially inseminate her, the plaintiff's lawyer, from the homosexual group Lambda Legal Defense Fund, said that the separation of church and state "principle ... needs to apply here."[3]

On the contrary, it is arbitrary nonsense to say that the principle should apply here. The state was not involved at all in the case. The case involves a private lesbian and private doctors practising in a private health facility. Even the lesbian's health plan was provided through a private company. The state was not an actor at any point in this situation. But, true to form, the manipulative anti-rational homosexual activists, do not care about the facts; they only care about finding the most

3. "Lesbian suing clinic for refusing to inseminate her: Physicians denied woman treatment for religious reasons," by Mary Vallis. *National Post*, October 14, 2005.

effective verbal levers to use to manipulate people's emotions to win support for their cause[4].

The homosexual attorney tries to make the principle stick by identifying the practice of medicine as part of the "public sphere." The extent to which socialism has become entrenched in mainstream America—and Canada—is evidenced by how easily people get away with this kind of claim. They assert that anything that is done in the presence of someone else is public as opposed to private. In one respect, that is true. But, in terms of philosophical categories, public is a reference to any aspect of life governed by the civil magistrate. Hence, private sector business activity does not take place in the public sphere. It is only by way of a passionately socialistic worldview that the jurisdiction of the state is expanded to include all activity that takes place in the presence of other people—an ideology which essentially places all business activity under the authority of an interventionist civil government.

So, when this LLDF attorney calls private medical practice part of the public sphere, she is either betraying her own ignorance; or she is using language strictly for its rhetorical and manipulative value; or she is identifying herself as a socialist, and once again revealing the philosophical interconnectedness between socialism, Secularism and the homosexual activist

4. The quintessential linguistic heist performed by homosexuals was to appropriate the word "gay." The homosexual activist mastery of rhetoric, however, does not end there. The use of "lifestyle" in place of something like "behaviour," as in "gay lifestyle" over against "homosexual behaviour," is another example. The example here, though, goes beyond linguistics to the level of philosophical paradigm and shows their effectiveness at using simple assertions based on their paradigm of thought, rarely being challenged, until their way of looking at the world becomes normative and the new basis from which debate takes place.

agenda.[5] And we discover that an assertion made by a socialist homosexual activist—that private medical practice is part of the public sphere—as though it is an objective, verifiable fact—an accurate representation of reality—is exposed as simply a notion derived from the pernicious ideology of socialism.

When a Christian holds to a high standard of reason and logic, and demands the same from those who would challenge him, he will find himself very lonely because it is a very rare Secularist—homosexual activist, or otherwise—who even cares to exercise a high level of reasoning ability in place of more effective tools such as verbal manipulation and censorship. When Secularists try to throw up the "separation of church and state" bogeyman, it is important to remember not to take them too seriously. And do not get spooked. They are the ones who are spooked; otherwise, they would not have raised the spectre of the "separation principle" in the first place.

Speaking more broadly about atheism, which is the philosophical basis for Secularism (as the extremists at the American Civil Liberties Union will tell you), popular U.S. conservative columnist Joseph Sobran, writes that "in itself [atheism] has no cohesive force. Whatever social cohesion it has provided so far has come more from its destructive hostility to the Christian civilization it has totally failed to improve on."[6] Atheism is not an ideology to fear.

5. You will notice that I identify the homosexual political agenda as one arm of the broader secularist agenda. From my reading, it appears that conservatives rarely, if ever, make this connection. *Ottawa Citizen* and *Western Standard* columnist, David Warren, however, did do so in his own way in October 2006. "For if I may contradict my allies on the socially conservative right, there was no 'homosexual agenda.' It is the old left agenda, being pursued for a moment by homosexual means." (David Warren, "Planning the Counter-Revolution," *Western Standard*, October 23, 2006, p. 13.)
6. Joseph Sobran, as cited in the *Federalist Digest*, July, 2006.

Let us turn now to a discussion of what the separation of church does not mean. It does not mean the separation of religion and politics. Secondly, it does not mean that politicians are banned from religious affiliations or that clergy have no right to speak about issues that have political relevance. Thirdly, separation of church and state does not mean that the two institutions have nothing at all to do with each other, as though they are capable of existing and operating without the one influencing the other.

The separation of religion and politics

The primary meaning behind the term separation of church and state when used by Secularists is the idea of the separation of religion from politics: religion, especially the Christian religion, has no business impacting public policy or legislation. In other words, they are operating under the faith vs. reason paradigm, a self-serving assumption whereby they convey the assertion that they are operating with reason, whereas those who hold to religious convictions are anti-rational, functioning by way of a "blind" faith. These Secularists believe that those who openly adhere to a religious outlook on life should keep their beliefs to themselves and not attempt to impose them on others. These Secularists also conveniently believe that their worldview is somehow morally neutral, and therefore qualifies as the philosophical foundation around which all competing interests can and must meet in order to carve out public policy and a social order that is acceptable to all. In terms of today's political rhetoric, one might call this hyper-pluralism.

Sometimes, Canada's establishment elites wear their philosophical illiteracy and anti-religious disposition on their sleeves. Such was the case with a 1999 ruling[7] by Ontario judge Robert Sharpe. The decision, on the right of Separate Schools to hire only Catholic teachers, protected the rights of the school board, but the reasoning was, well, unreasonable! "A non-believer would necessarily teach the subject from an intellectual rather than a faith-based perspective," Justice Sharpe wrote. If there is any evidence at all of "systemic discrimination" in Canadian society today, it's this entrenched bigotry against Christianity that sees it as simply a matter of fact that our faith is not intellectual—or rational.

The extent of intellectual immaturity, not to mention the litany of logical fallacies, in this Secularist worldview is so great that one is tempted to dismiss it out of hand and move on to more productive and intellectually stimulating endeavours. Nevertheless, in view of the impact of Secular Humanist thinking on the Canadian enterprise, it is important to confront this errant worldview, and expose some of the particulars of this anti-rational outlook. [8]

One has to begin by observing that Secular Humanism is a stridently bigoted ideology with a special, and sometimes even visceral, hostility towards Christianity and Christians. When Secularists object to religion in politics, almost without exception they have Christianity in mind. The government of Liberal Prime Minister Jean Chrétien did not have any problem banning references to Jesus at a memorial service for the victims of a downed aircraft off Nova Scotia, yet non-Christian religions were not similarly censored.[9] Prime Minister Jean

7. Daly v. Ontario (Attorney General)
8. Iain Benson identifies some important examples of the absurd reasoning used by Secularist judges in his article, "Notes Towards A (Re)Definition of the 'Secular'," 2005. Most of you probably have two-year-olds who would be embarrassed if they were caught entertaining the kind of mindless notions and twisted logic evident in the thinking of these Canadian judges.
9. "Christianity's once strong influences in danger of being plowed under," by Joseph Woodard. *Calgary Herald*, August 14, 1999.

Chrétien avoided references to Christianity in his comments at a memorial service for the victims of the 9/11 terrorist attack on America[10], but his successor, Paul Martin, included a Native Indian cleansing ceremony as part of his swearing-in festivities as Prime Minister[11]. You also see much more sensitivity to Islam in Canadian non-discrimination policy than towards Christians. Sikhs can wear their turbans in place of the traditional RCMP headdress[12] and a Sikh student even won the right to wear his ceremonial dagger—kirpan—at school[13] despite the post-9/11 sensitivity to public safety.

Canadians must understand that Secular Humanist ideology is not a dry, sterile worldview. It is not academic, cerebral or particularly intellectual. Secular Humanism is dynamic and passionate—and if leading secularists' treatment of Christianity is anything by which to judge, one of the dominant passions of their ideology is hatred, whether they recognize this to be the case or not.[14] If this is a central characteristic of Secularism, it is absurd that Secular Humanists claim to be the party of reason, while accusing Christians of being driven by an irrational faith. These assertions run parallel to the claims that Secularism promotes peace and tolerance while Christianity

10. "Recall Jean Chrétien's boast that banning any form of prayer from Canada's 9/11 memorial service was the 'best decision' he had ever made." "God came back a long time ago," By Fr. Raymond J. De Souza. *National Post*, August 7, 2004.

11. "Liberal heebee-jeebies," by Alexander Panetta. April 5, 2004. http://paulmartintime.ca/mediacoverage/000422.html. "Scrapped bill no great victory yet for First Nations," by Sarah Petrescu.
The Martlet, January 15, 2004.

12. This development came in 1990 in a ruling by Solicitor General, Pierre Cadieux, who said, "Today, I'm announcing the government's decision which is not only the correct one in law but also the right decision." This followed a 1986 decision permitting Sikhs in the Metro Toronto police force to wear Turbans while on duty. See "Sikhs and their Turban" at http://www.sikhmarg.com/english/sikh-turban.html.

13. "A sharp decision." *The Ottawa Citizen*, March 3, 2006

14. Certainly in terms of the growing acceptance for the fluid and expanding definition of "hatred" used by homosexual activists today, it would be impossible for Secularists to credibly argue that the outcome of their approach towards Christians and the Christian ethic of liberty reflects anything but hatred towards Christianity.

is a threat proportionate to that of Islamo-fascism[15] or Hitler's genocidal religion.

Take note of the following astonishing comment by David Rudenstine, the dean of the Benjamin N. Cardozo Law School at Yeshiva University (and formerly an attorney for the ACLU [American Civil Liberties Union]) from an address in June 2005 to 200 undergraduate university counsellors: "Faith challenges the underpinnings of legal education. Faith is a willingness to accept belief in things for which we have no evidence, or which runs counter to evidence we have. Faith does not tolerate opposing views, does not acknowledge inconvenient facts. Law schools stand in fundamental opposition to this."[16]

Another remarkable comment comes in a British Columbia court ruling. In a decision by the B.C. Court of Appeal against Christian public school teacher Chris Kempling, the court ruled that Mr. Kempling was guilty of (illegitimate) discrimination against homosexuals in some of his writings.[17] This, despite the fact that some of those comments were based on statistics from the *New England Journal of Medicine* and the Atlanta

15. Lesbian talk-show host, Rosie O'Donnell, in late 2006, equated Christians with the 9/11 terrorists. "Radical Christianity is just as threatening as radical Islam in a country like America..." she said while discussing the 9/11 anniversary and the war in Iraq. "Rosie's View: 'Radical Christians' Same as 9/11 Terrorists," by Jeff Johnson. CNSNews.com, September 14, 2006. http://www.cnsnews.com/ViewCulture.asp?Page=/Culture/archive/200609/CUL20060914a.html. Homosexual singer Elton John bested Ms. O'Donnell a couple of months later with his profound assessment that "Religion promotes the hatred and spite against gays.... From my point of view I would ban religion completely. Organised religion doesn't work. It turns people into really hateful lemmings and it's not really compassionate." "Elton: religion breeds gay hatred," by Nicholas Christian. Scotsman, November 12, 2006. http://news.scotsman.com/celebrities.cfm?id=1674402006.
16. "Collision Course; Secular Justifications; New Religious Schools; 'Reasonable Faith.'" by Thomas Adcock. *The New York Law Journal*, June 17, 2005, p. 16.
17. Kempling v. British Columbia College of Teachers. June 13, 2005. Docket: CA031628. http://www.courts.gov.bc.ca/jdb-txt/ca/05/03/2005bcca0327err1.htm.

Centers for Disease Control[18] and were, therefore, rooted in scientific research, not religious dogma. This is just one of many examples of Secular partisans in Canada placing themselves at odds with science. In fact, Canada's Secularist legal system, from the law schools right up to the Supreme Court of Canada bench, is one of the best places to find flaming religious fanatics who despise scientific research when the evidence contravenes their religious orientation and "sacred" cows.

On the other hand, Chris Kempling's case stands as one out of many in which intelligent Christianity advances a view that is aligned with science. The absurdity of seeing Secularism as scientifically responsible and Christianity as anti-rational will one day be seen as one of the most interesting intellectual curiosities of 20th and 21st century thought.

A statement by Lambda Legal Defense Fund lawyer, Jennifer Pizer, regarding the California lawsuit against two doctors who refused to provide artificial insemination to a lesbian, demonstrates the shocking arrogance of Secularism, and the unswerving resolve of the homosexual lobby to crush the public expression of Christianity: "These physicians, or anyone else who is operating a business, are free to worship as they will and believe as they will, but not to put those beliefs into action in a way that harms other people in the public sphere."[19]

simply to refuse to provide artificial insemination ← *the harm was*

18. Corey, L. & Holmes, K., "Sexual transmission of hepatitis A in homosexual men." *New England Journal of Medicine*, 1980, 302, 435-438; Centers for Disease Control, "Facts about recent trends in reported U.S. AIDS cases." Atlanta: Centers for Disease Control 1994).
19. "Lesbian suing clinic for refusing to inseminate her: Physicians denied woman treatment for religious reasons," by Mary Vallis. *National Post*, October 14, 2005.

Conservative Jewish columnist Don Feder did not pull any punches in a column he wrote on the hatred of the left, or Secularists, to Christianity in May 2005[20]. His context is the United States, which parallels the situation in Canada to a great degree.

Since the founding of the Moral Majority in the late 1970s, the Left has been obsessed with conservative Christians. This fixation is driven by fear, loathing, and old-fashioned opportunism. Hatred of traditional Christians is as old as H.L. Mencken (who, by the way, didn't have the warm fuzzies for blacks or Jews either). In recent decades, the Left has come to see evangelical Christians as the principal obstacle to the realization of its social agenda, hence the embodiment of evil. Correspondingly, attacks on "fundamentalists" have grown increasingly shrill. Even so, the rhetoric of the past two weeks has taken the anti-religious right *jihad* to new depths.

Last week, Colorado Senator Ken Salazar (a Democrat, naturally) told a radio interviewer that Dr. James Dobson and Focus on the Family "are the Antichrist of the world" for urging citizens to demand their senators vote to end the filibuster of Bush judges... Salazar later amended himself to say Focus and Dobson's "approach was un-Christian, meaning self-serving and selfish." In effect, Salazar is saying that for a Christian group to attempt to get government to reflect Christian values is "un-Christian."...

Repeating a mantra of the Secular Left, Salazar warned, "What has happened here (Christian political activism

20. "The Left's 'Dominionist' Demons," by Don Feder. FrontPageMagazine.com, May 5, 2005.

on behalf of Bush judicial nominees) is there has been a hijacking of the U.S. Senate by what I call the religious right-wing of the country." When any other group (environmentalists, feminists, peace activists) organizes to effect political change through education, lobbying, and get-out-the-vote efforts, it's called... democracy. When Christians (as Christians) try to exercise their rights as citizens, it's called sinister, an attempted hijacking of the political process—theocracy!...

Salazar's shrill and inflammatory rhetoric also appears in the superficial and puerile writings of Canada's mainstream media when they report on the progress that social conservatives make within the institutional structure of the Conservative Party of Canada. In mid-2005, Frances Russell wrote a column on this subject for the *Winnipeg Free Press*[21]. She wrote:

What worries a clear majority of Canadians is a peculiarly American strain of Christianity that clamours for its own religious freedom and rights, but squelches them for others. It seeks political power for the express purpose of remaking the nation in its own rigid and authoritarian image.... This destruction of everything liberal democracy is supposed to stand for is a key reason Stephen Harper's Conservatives are sliding in the polls even as the Liberals plumb new depths of ethical and possibly criminal misbehaviour. Last week, the *Globe and Mail* carried several articles on the Christian Right's successful capture of at least eight Conservative nominations in B.C., Ontario and Atlantic Canada. These candidates all have ties to the U.S. evangelical Christian movements now commanding the

21. "Christians capturing Tory party," by Francis Russell. *Winnipeg Free Press*, June 3, 2005.

heights of the Republican Party. Focus on the Family and Promise Keepers talk glibly about openness and caring. But what they are really about is enforcing discrimination and patriarchy.

On May 30, 2005, Sean Gordon writing in the left-wing *Toronto Star*, said: "The Conservative party's nomination procedures have left it vulnerable to special interest groups, a flaw some long-time activists worry could reinforce negative stereotypes about the party. Some Tories fret that a recent flurry of nominations has elected several socially conservative candidates who may provide more fuel to Liberal criticisms of the party.... Moderates within the party have recently raised concerns that fundamentalist Christian organizations have succeeded in winning control over a clutch of riding associations in B.C., Ontario and Nova Scotia. In those ridings, candidates with ties to groups like the Christian Legal Defence Fund, Focus on the Family—which is affiliated with a well-funded U.S. organization of the same name—and to evangelical churches won nominations with the support of high-profile pastors."[22]

These secularists aren't afraid of using deception to push their agenda. They know people will rarely investigate their comments. Take the case of *Ottawa Citizen* columnist Janice Kennedy, who wrote a diatribe condemning social conservatives for supposedly hijacking the terms "marriage" and "family," and using them for their own narrow, ideological advantage. Her column was a pathetic piece of writing and McGill professor, Doug Farrow, was one person who took her to task, exposing her antics.

22. "Tory image in peril, some fear," by Sean Gordon. *Toronto Star*, May 30, 2005.

Citizen columnist Janice Kennedy ("'Family' Heist," Feb. 26, 2006) detected... linguistic skulduggery by the revolutionary groups.... The word they have purloined is... "family," which they have arbitrarily attached to their own radical model: the triadic model of father, mother and offspring. Ms. Kennedy quoted against them the third edition of The American Heritage Dictionary, which gives this definition of family: "two or more people who share goals and values, have long-term commitments to one another, and reside usually in the same dwelling place." That, she implied, is the traditional meaning, which is being undermined by the bigotry of those whose "slick twisting of perfectly good words ... into ugly shapes" is the result of spiteful and intolerant mindsets.

But who exactly is guilty of this charge? In Kennedy's attempt to demonize her opponents, she didn't mention that her definition is a secondary one. The primary definition offered by the same dictionary is "a fundamental social group in society typically consisting of a man and woman and their offspring." The definition Kennedy touts as traditional is not mentioned in the original edition. Nor does the Oxford English Dictionary offer any support for her thesis that the word has been stolen by "ultra-conservative crusaders" who are advancing "agendas dominated by discrimination and an exclusionary world-view." Au contraire, a stroll through the dictionaries suggests that it is Kennedy who is attempting a word-heist; or, as I would say, playing the Bolshevik-Menshevik game.[23]

23. "The Bolshevik-Menshevik game," by Douglas Farrow. *The Ottawa Citizen*, March 15, 2006. What Prof. Farrow means by the Bolshevik-Menshevik game, he explains earlier in this article regarding Lenin's tactics to gain control over the Social Democrats in the run-up to the Russian Revolution.

Even more recently, the Liberal Party of Canada's interim leader Bill Graham, wallowed in the mire when he launched several days of bigoted attacks in the House of Commons against a Christian employed by the Minister of the Environment. Darrel Reid was formerly head of Focus on the Family Canada and, prior to that, chief of staff to Preston Manning when he was the leader of the Official Opposition as leader of the Reform Party. Mr. Reid also has a Ph.D. in history from Queen's University.

Bill Graham's condemnation of the Conservative Environment Minister for hiring Mr. Reid was launched during Question Period in the House of Commons, but was repeated outside the Commons, where he called Mr. Reid's pro-marriage views "Neanderthal."

Mr. Graham never explained how Mr. Reid's pro-family views had any bearing on his role in an environmental portfolio. Of course, he couldn't. Mr. Graham was simply reflecting the view that vocal Christians aren't sufficiently civilized to qualify as legitimate candidates for high-level government employment. At the very least, he was demonstrating that Christians are legitimate targets for Liberals to "objectify" and exploit with bigoted and hateful rhetoric in order to score political points.

Joseph Ben-Ami, the Jewish executive director of the Institute for Canadian Values, said Mr. Graham's attack was "out of bounds." "The fact that he would feel that… he was somehow fulfilling some sort of public good by figuratively lynching a guy because of his strong Christian beliefs—that he could do that with impunity—is a mark of how badly deteriorated our sense of propriety has become in this country."[24] That's putting it mildly!

An American rabbi has also recently talked about the increasingly unrestrained hatred of that country's Secularists against Christianity.[25] "Consider the long list of anti-Christian books that have been published in recent months," wrote Rabbi Daniel Lapin, an author and Jewish community leader, and president of the national organization Toward Tradition. "Here are just a few samples of more than 30 similar titles, all from mainstream publishers:

> "American Fascists: The Christian Right and the
> War on America"
> "The Baptizing of America: The Religious
> Right's Plans for the Rest of Us"
> "The End of Faith: Religion, Terror, and the
> Future of Reason"
> "Piety & Politics: The Right-wing Assault on
> Religious Freedom"
> "Atheist Universe: The Thinking Person's
> Answer to Christian Fundamentalism"
> "Thy Kingdom Come: How the Religious Right
> Distorts the Faith and Threatens America"
> "Religion Gone Bad: The Hidden Dangers
> of the Christian Right"

"What is truly alarming is that there are more of these books for sale at your local large book store warning against the perils of fervent Christianity than those warning against the perils of fervent Islam."

24. "Government appointee attacked for his beliefs," by Frank Stirk. *Christian Week*, November 1, 2006.
25. "A rabbi's warning to U.S. Christians," by Rabbi Daniel Lapin. WorldNetDaily.com, January 13, 2007.

One of these recent books was written by Richard Dawkins, a wild-eyed disciple of the atheist religion. Jonathan Kay, commenting on Mr. Dawkins's book in the *National Post*, wrote, "Atheism has been an accepted creed in the West since the French Revolution. But surely its champions weren't always this obnoxious. A new breed of bestselling atheistic jihadis seeks not only to declare God dead, Nietzsche-style, but to proclaim everyone who believes in Him a pathetic, deluded imbecile."

To illustrate his point, Mr. Kay cited a compelling example of Mr. Dawkins' scientific sophistication: Mr. Dawkins "dismisses the deity we know from the Old Testament as 'arguably the most unpleasant character in all fiction... a petty, unjust, unforgiving control freak, a vindictive bloodthirsty ethnic cleanser, a misogynistic, homophobic, racist, infanticidal, genocidal, filicidal, pestilential, megalomaniacal, sadomasochistic, capriciously malevolent bully'." A drunken sailor would be hard-pressed to provide us with a more choice example of verbal vomit.

It is clear: Secularism is not benign; on the contrary, it inspires bigotry and the hatred of Christians.

Intimidating Christians out of the public square

Homosexual Secularists are some of the most bigoted and hateful towards Christians. One could write a separate book just illustrating the examples of this growing hostility in the past few years in Canada and elsewhere. A handful of these attacks on Christians have come from police officers, shattering people's confidence in the ability of the justice system to treat people fairly, and raising the spectre of the

Gestapo. Even passive expressions of discriminatory justice, such as when police and crown prosecutors refuse to prosecute homosexuals for public nudity when others would face charges, undermines confidence in the justice system. And what are we to make of pictures of anti-marriage judges partying hard with homosexual activists in the midst of the marriage definition battles[26] or Chief Justice Roy McMurtry of the Ontario Court of Appeal not recusing himself from Ontario's homosexual "marriage" case, *Halpern and the Attorney General of Canada,* despite having a lesbian daughter who was living in a homosexual union.[27]

A prime example of the extremism and bigotry of the homosexual activist wing of Secular Humanism is the fight to oppose raising the age of sexual consent from 14 to 16. Despite cross-party support for this very moderate child protection initiative, including from the International Socialists'-affiliated New Democrats, homosexual activists condemn the Conservative Party proposal. These self-anointed defenders of Canada's new (im)morality have organised, not to give young people greater access to education or health care or new apprenticeship opportunities; these sex fanatics want to give these children greater rights to unrestricted sex. There's a priority that resonates with civility and social responsibility!

Interestingly, as reported in Ottawa's homosexual paper *Capital Xtra,*[28] Peter Bochove of the quaintly named Committee to Abolish the 19th Century criticized the impact

---

26. "Judges Party with Homosexual Activists." Reality, July/August 2003.
    http://www.realwomenca.com/newsletter/2003_july_aug/article_4.html.
27. REAL Women of Canada has filed a complaint with the Canadian Judicial Council alleging judicial misconduct by Justice McMurtry for not recusing himself. You can read their case on their website at http://www.realwomenca.com/press.htm#07_17_06 or contact REAL Women at (613) 236-4001.
28. ["Rights groups to tell Parliament to keep consent at 14," Gareth Kirkby. *Capital Xtra,* January 11, 2007. http://www.xtra.ca/public/viewstory.aspx?AFF_TYPE=2&STORY_ID=2534&PUB_TEMPLATE_ID=2]

of fairy-tales on public policy. But he wasn't talking about Secular Humanism or the supposed benefits of improving access to child sex. Remarkably, this mild-mannered, even-handed activist was condemning Christian politicians whose moral convictions appear to have an impact on the views they bring to the public policy process. "I think people are entitled to believe any fairy-tale that they wish," he said, "and if it gives them comfort, that's great. But they should keep it in their church, not my Parliament."

But this "spiritual" heir of Pol Pot and Hitler went even further: he said—and *Capital Xtra* printed—that these conservative Christians should actually be banned from pursuing elected office: "And that's why they don't belong in government." That's the mentality of this sex-obsessed member of Canada's homosexual "mainstream" who has white-washed the risk to children from sexual exploitation in order to advance his dishonest and child-endangering political agenda. These wild-eyed extremists wouldn't last five minutes under the scrutiny of ordinary Canadians—which is probably why the pro-homosexualist, pro-Secular Humanist mainstream media does not publicize their inflammatory rhetoric.

When the principle of equality before the law is replaced by special treatment for favoured groups, then civility has been replaced by barbarianism, and freedom has been replaced by the gulag. Public officials should not be surprised if recent cases start generating questions among the general public about whether or not people with any history in homosexual activism should automatically be banned from employment in the police force.

One of the most recent—and offensive—examples of Christian-hating has been at the hands of Scotland's Gay

Police Association. They produced an ad for *The Independent*, a national newspaper in Scotland, which showed a Bible next to a pool of blood with the headline "In the name of the father." Beside the picture was the claim that a rise in homophobic attacks was due to religious intolerance: "In the last 12 months, the GPA has recorded a 74% increase in homophobic incidents, where the sole or primary motivating factor was the religious belief of the perpetrator."[29]

Scotland Yard investigated the incident as a "hate crime," or what they are calling a "faith crime." It should also be investigating these thugs for fraud. Unfortunately, for some strange reason, Christians do not make more of an issue regarding these accusations of hate. Any honest person who has examined the various physical assaults against homosexuals knows that the demographic for those who attack homosexuals is almost completely different from the Christian demographic. The claim that Christian teaching against homosexuality is the source of danger to homosexuals, or provides an environment conducive to harming homosexuals, is fraudulent at its root and is itself an expression of fanatical hatred and intolerance.[30]

29. "British Gay Police Association Investigated by Scotland Yard for Anti-Christian Ad," by Hilary White. LifeSiteNews.com, July 21, 2006. See a picture of the ad at http://www.cnsnews.com/storyimages/2006/060725rhBritishHomosexualPoliceAd.jpg.

30. An August 19, 2006 article in *The New Mexican* ("Edgewood: Four indicted in gay-bashing case," by John Sena. http://www.freenewmexican.com/news/48092.html) reported on a case of "gay-bashing" of an 18-year-old at a party following which four people were charged with kidnapping, aggravated battery, conspiracy and false imprisonment. Christians? Yeah, right! On August 6, 2006, *The Washington Post* reported on a case of vandalism to a homosexual couple's home in Virginia ("Vandalism Damages More Than Property; For Gay Couple, Fear Hits Home"). On August 9, 2006, *The Windsor Star* reported on an 18-year-old Detroit teen being sentenced to 12 years in jail for shooting a homosexual Windsor man ("Victim's family asks: 'Why?': Teen gets 8 to 12 years for shooting gay man," by Dalson Chen). If any case could be made for this man having a religious motivation, it would have been all over the news. But not one word along those lines. On June 21, *The Edmonton Sun* reported on a case of "gay-bashing" in which the perpetrator was at the time "living on the street, abusing booze and drugs and living like a punk" ("Reformed gay basher avoids jail term," by Tony Blais). This is the consistent witness of history: Christians do not beat up homosexuals, notwithstanding the fraudulent slurs endemic to the wild-eyed homosexual activist movement.

Gay Police Association Officer David Lyle has responded to criticism, claiming that the ad was published by the association "in order to highlight a serious social issue," adding that "The GPA article and statement in *The Independent* only sought to highlight the facts. The article does not claim or infer that any religion is to blame for this increase. It does state clearly that it was the individuals themselves who commit these crimes who have used their faith to legitimize their actions. People cannot be allowed to hide behind the cloak of religion as an excuse to commit hate crimes."

Anyone can claim anything as a cover for his actions. If the GPA is going to make inflammatory statements, they should be based on facts, not conjecture, assumption and unproven assertions. The GPA's comments more closely resemble an agenda of intimidation and brainwashing more than anything that could be mistaken for a contribution to intelligent, civil debate.

Thankfully, the Catholic Church in Scotland has forthrightly condemned this incident as "outrageous and intolerant," with Peter Kearney, spokesman for the Scottish bishops, noting that, "This is exactly the kind of intolerance that gay groups claim they are trying to clamp down on…. Once again, it is the Christian Bible which has been singled out with a headline which has Christian connections. It is another sign that Christianphobia has become fashionable and acceptable."[31]

Even Scottish Parliamentarians are condemning the bigotry. "In Scotland, a member of the Holyrood parliament tabled a motion condemning the Gay Police Association for publishing

31. "Church Backs Scotland Yard Enquiry into Gay 'Hate Crime' Advert." *Christian Today*, August 15, 2006. http://www.christiantoday.com/news/society/church.backs.scotland.yard. investigation.into.gay.hate.crime.advert/1022.htm.

a 'Christianophobic advertisement' in a national newspaper, explains *Total Catholic*. Murdo Fraser, MSP for Mid Scotland and Fife, launched the motion and has said that the parliament 'rejects this assertion as totally erroneous; values Scotland's Christian community and the contribution it makes to our society and our culture; deeply regrets that any police officer would choose to place an advertisement in any medium to make such a gratuitous insult to a section of the Scottish population; and hopes that the all (sic) police officers will act in a manner that reflects fully the attitudes, values and beliefs which Scotland, as a modern society founded on the Christian faith (sic)'."[32]

This is the kind of push-back that we should have seen in Canada with what ended up as a successful attempt to pass hate crime legislation here. Bill C-250 was introduced by intolerant, socialist Member of Parliament Svend Robinson, and passed with the support of then Prime Minister, Jean Chrétien. The New Democrat was Canada's first openly homosexual MP, and he used the same kind of dishonest rhetoric to claim that Christian opposition to homosexuality was a significant cause of harassment against homosexuals. Of course, to provide cover for these kinds of slurs, homosexual activists lump all forms of opposition to homosexuality together, treating the assault and murder of homosexuals and the denial of government benefits or employment to homosexuals as equivalent to the criticism of homosexuality, whether for theological, medical or social reasons.

Why Christians and other social conservatives have allowed homosexual activists to get away with this kind of rhetorical sleight of hand remains unclear. At any rate, it continues

32. Ibid.

today, and it helps cultivate an environment in which the general public has become more open to censorship and the elimination of free speech because they think that too much freedom leads to dead and abused homosexuals.

Another example of the kind of police-initiated bigotry that can develop in this kind of environment comes from Florida. "A homosexual-activist police officer assigned to security at a Promise Keepers men's conference in Florida is being investigated for threatening members of a Christian organization petitioning for a state constitutional marriage amendment," reported WorldNetDaily in August 2006.[33]

The Florida Family Policy Council had rented a display table at the June Promise Keepers conference in the Fort Lauderdale area to publicize its petition signature drive for a vote in Florida in defence of real marriage. "But as the signatures were being collected, officers of the Sunrise city police department ordered volunteers for Florida4Marriage.org to stop accepting names. 'Officers then physically removed the petitions from 'public view' on the table at the exhibitors tent,' the council said in a website update of the situation. 'Two of the male officers mocked the volunteers by kissing each other after they initially removed all the petitions from the area'."[34]

Thankfully, officials are investigating the incident. "In the actual confrontation," according to WorldNetDaily, "[John] Stemberger [the president and general counsel of the Florida

33. "Homosexual-activist cop threatens Christians." WorldNetDaily.com, August 4, 2006.
    http://www.wnd.com/news/article.asp?ARTICLE_ID=51378.

34. Ibid.

Family Policy Council] was called after the officers removed the petitions. He sought further legal counsel from Rick Nelson of American Liberties Institute and then confronted Sgt. [Stephen] Allen. He said he asked the sergeant what law or ordinance was being violated by the petitions and Allen simply responded with a not-entirely accurate lecture on Jesus' view of homosexuality in the New Testament and the statement that the petition was a 'waste of time.' The sergeant then proclaimed he was the authority and 'the Bible says that Christians should obey the authorities'."[35]

"I have never in my life seen such unprofessional and bizarre behavior from a law enforcement officer," said Mr. Stemberger. "This kind of ridiculous harassment and intimidation was meant to thwart the effort to protect marriage in Florida. It should remind all of us that we are engaged in a culture war…"

Stemberger told WorldNetDaily that he filed his complaint with internal affairs. "They are doing a good-faith investigation because they've called me several times. I know that the officer's retained counsel…. No one would have ever believed our story without that photograph. That photograph really captures the attitude that we were approached with."

Stemberger added that without a significant result from the police department's investigation, it would produce a "chilling" effect on any Christian activities in public areas. And Promise Keepers spokesman Steve Chavis told WND, "We always have great relationships with the venues and the security details (at the conferences) and that's the first time we ever saw that level of partisanship from security."

35. Ibid.

Unfortunately, however, this is the kind of behaviour Christians should expect to face more and more in the future. This Florida incident follows a case in Pennsylvania that took place in October 2004. In that case, four Christian protesters who demonstrated at a Philadelphia homosexual event were arrested and charged with offences that carried up to 47 years of jail time. Reporting on the story again in December 2004, WorldNetDaily wrote: "As WorldNetDaily reported, on Oct. 10, the group was 'preaching God's Word' to a crowd of people attending the outdoor Philadelphia 'OutFest' event and displaying banners with biblical messages. After a confrontation with a group called the Pink Angels, described by protesters as 'a militant mob of homosexuals,' the 11 Christians were arrested and spent a night in jail. Eight charges were filed: criminal conspiracy, possession of instruments of crime, reckless endangerment of another person, ethnic intimidation, riot, failure to disperse, disorderly conduct and obstructing highways. None of the Pink Angels was cited or arrested."[36]

Repent America issued their own press release, noting that, "Repent America obeyed all laws, and even the unlawful requests, to move by the Philadelphia Civil Affairs police officers in an effort of co-operation. Regardless of Repent America's compliance, Chief James Tiano, head of the Civil Affairs Unit, without warning, ordered the arrests of the Christians and hauled them off to jail, where they spent 21 hours, before being released the following day. Ten Christians were individually charged with three felonies and five misdemeanors, while a teenager with the group was charged with a misdemeanor."[37]

36. "Prosecutor: Bible is 'fighting words'". WorldNetDaily.com (December 16, 2004). http://www.worldnetdaily.com/news/article.asp?ARTICLE_ID=41969.
37. "Christians Arrested". (October 11, 2004). http://www.covenantnews.com/repent041012.htm.

On February 18, 2005, Justice Pamela Dembe dismissed the outstanding charges against these Repent America protestors. Condemning the prosecutor's anti-American push to censor Christians, Justice Dembe said, in her decision: "This is one of the very few countries that protects unpopular speech. We cannot stifle speech because we don't want to hear it or we don't want to hear it now."[38] Repent America also noted that,

> "At a previous hearing, after watching the 22-minute videotape of the events leading to the defendants' arrests, Judge Dembe dissolved an order prohibiting the men from being within one hundred feet of a homosexual event, saying, it "is an unreasonable restriction on a person's right to speak," and admitted that their actions "did not amount to criminal behavior", and recommended that those who wish not to hear the speech move to another country."[39]

In another incident, on July 16, 2006, "three members of the evangelical group Repent America say they were handcuffed and arrested by Chicago police officers for passing out Christian literature to homosexuals and holding up signs with Bible verses near Navy Pier"[40] during the city's "Gay Games."

"Repent America filed an emergency motion for a temporary restraining order. Consequently, the Metropolitan Pier and Exposition Authority—the government agency that runs Navy

38. "Philadelphia prosecutor drowns in sea of constitutionally protected freedoms". Repent America (February 18, 2005). http://www.repentamerica.com/pr_prosecutiondrowns.html.
39. Ibid.
40. "Suit Filed On Behalf of Repent America Members Arrested in Chicago," by Jim Brown. AgapePress (July 20, 2006). http://headlines.agapepress.org/archive/7/202006b.asp. Cf. "Charges Against Chicago Police's Violation of Civil and First Amendment Rights at Gay Games Moving Forward." December 19, 2006. http://www.christiannewswire.com/news/796931783.html.

Pier—agreed to allow the Christian group to continue their activity there. However, Chicago attorney John Mauck says the arresting officers had made it clear, at least one of them in profane language, that Repent America's message was not welcome."[41]

The Christians' lawyer believes it was because of this very message that the three ministry members were targeted. The lawsuit he has filed on behalf of the arrested believers alleges that their free-speech rights were violated by the city and by the police officers.

In Canada, of course, there was the incident in April 2004 in which homosexual activists calling themselves The Gay Militia raided a private meeting of Christians who were raising funds in support of youth pastor Steven Boissoin.[42] Most of these thugs had their faces covered, and they were carrying weapons—sticks—and chanting and banging their sticks together in order to disrupt the meeting and to intimidate the audience, a substantial number of whom were senior citizens.

After a one-and-a-half-year investigation, only one of these thugs was convicted and his penalty was a paltry $500 fine.[43] This was probably better than nothing, which is the result most Christians were expecting, but it was nevertheless a pathetic sentence. This decision demonstrates how far along the campaign is to rid Canada's justice system of the principle of equality. If the roles were reversed, and it was Christians— or any group of people opposed to homosexuality—raiding a

41. Ibid.
42. Boissoin is facing a human rights prosecution over criticism of homosexuality that he has voiced in Alberta newspapers in his role as a youth pastor, calling young people out of lives of despair and sin, and to follow Christ.
43. "Activist guilty in 'gay' disturbance: Boisterous group invades Christian coalition's dinner," by Daryl Slade. *Calgary Herald*, October 29, 2005.

homosexual meeting, there would have been a media frenzy for days, the police would have been pressured to launch a speedy investigation, activists would have demanded prosecution to the full extent of the law. Human rights complaints would have been launched as well as the criminal prosecution, and there would have been demands that "hate" be considered as an exacerbating factor at sentencing in order to increase the sentence that the culprits would have faced if found guilty of the charges laid against them.

Not in this case, though, because secular humanism despises Christianity so it is prepared to tolerate all kinds of assaults against Christians and their faith, even at the expense of principles of fundamental justice such as the most basic commitment to equal treatment before the law. It cannot be stated often enough: Secular Humanists despise the principle of equality before the law, as does the homosexual activist wing of Secular Humanism.

A more recent case of anti-Christian violence took place against a Catholic city councillor in British Columbia. "Homophobia, die" was scrawled on the door of his barber shop in June 2006.[44] No one has been charged yet for the crime so we don't know if it was committed by a homosexual or a fellow traveler. The Kamloops councillor, John DeCicco, expressed opposition to the city's Gay Pride Week proclamation. In the past he has referred to homosexuality as "not normal and not natural." About his opposition to making a Gay Pride Week proclamation, he said "I'm not against lesbian and gay people, but I don't agree that I should have to endorse it." One would be hard pressed to find condemnation of this criminal act by

44. "'Homophobia Die' Scrawled on Door of City Councillor Who Opposed Gay Pride," by John-Henry Westen. LifeSiteNews.com, June 16, 2006

one or more homosexualists. Tolerance and respect do not seem to come naturally to many homosexual activists.

Canada's human rights commissions and tribunals have been among the most dangerous weapons wielded against pro-family Canadians. Rapidly taken over by radical pandering socialists, they were co-opted by the homosexual movement's "anti-discrimination" agenda. They have been appropriately caricatured in recent years as "homosexual rights commissions." It is typically to the human rights commissions that homosexuals appeal cases of alleged discrimination. This is how homosexuals drove their agenda in the past decade at the expense of people like Christian print shop owner Scott Brockie,[45] B.C. teacher Chris Kempling, Saskatchewan newspaper advertiser Hugh Owens,[46] a marriage commissioner in Saskatchewan,[47] mayors who refused to issue "Gay Pride" proclamations[48] and the Knights of Columbus.[49]

Homosexual cases, however, are only a symptom of the broader anti-Christian ideology that under girds the human rights commission agenda, as noted by the *National Post*'s managing editor, Jonathan Kay.[50]

... In a handful of unusual but disturbing cases, complainants have sought to transform them into

45. "If Chapters can ban immoral writing, why can't a printer refuse to print it?," by Terry O'Neill. *Report* magazine, January 7, 2002.
46. "High court reserves ruling on biblical scriptures," by Anne Kyle. *The Regina Leader-Post*, September 16, 2005. "Appeal court decision worries gay activists: Human rights board finding overturned in Scripture ad case," by Anne Kyle. *The Saskatoon StarPhoenix*, April 15, 2006.
47. "Saskatchewan Marriage Commissioner under Investigation for Unwillingness to Perform Gay 'Marriages'". LifeSiteNews.com, July 14, 2005.
48. "Controversial ex-mayor seeking Tory nomination," by Gloria Galloway. *The Globe and Mail*, October 19, 2006.
49. "Gay zealots are looking for more than tolerance," by Dan Gardner. *Victoria Times-Colonist*, December 4, 2005.
50. "Censorship in the name of 'human rights'," by Jonathan Kay . *National Post*, April 3, 2006.

an instrument of censorship and social engineering. Several years ago, for instance, a Saskatchewan human rights board of inquiry ruled against Regina resident Hugh Owens, who'd placed ads in the *Saskatoon StarPhoenix* citing biblical passages decrying homosexuality alongside an image of two stick-figure men holding hands, with a diagonal line running through the pair. An "=" sign appeared between the verse references and the drawing, making it clear that Owens was making a religious point. ("I put the biblical references, but not the actual verses, so the ad would become interactive," Owens later said. "I figured somebody would have to look them up in the Bible first.") Nonetheless, the human-rights panel fined Owens for promoting "hatred." In essence, the Bible was declared hate speech in the name of human rights.

Last August, a similar case went before the Alberta Human Rights Commission. This time, the object of censorship was Calgary's Bishop, Fred Henry, who'd publicly articulated the traditional Christian injunction against homosexual behaviour, and called on the government to use its "coercive power" to stop same-sex marriage. (The complainants withdrew the case once the media were done with the story.)

Last month, an equally spurious complaint was lodged in Alberta. Syed Soharwardy, the Saudi-trained leader of the "Islamic Supreme Council of Canada," claims the republication of the Danish cartoons of the Prophet Mohammed by the Calgary-based *Western Standard* magazine "created unbearable stress, humiliation and insult." Soharwardy is not a particularly sympathetic plaintiff. He insists that Palestinians seeking "independence" are not terrorists, but more akin to "freedom fighters." And his literature contains absurdities such as "what Israeli forces are doing to Palestinians is worse than the Holocaust." But no matter: The Alberta Human Rights and Citizenship Commission accepted his complaint, and the matter is now in the conciliation phase. Rather than give in and apologize for its editors' thought crime, the Standard hired a lawyer to help draft a response. If the case goes to investigation and then appeal, it could drag on for years and cost the magazine tens of thousands of dollars. But because this isn't real litigation, Soharwardy himself hasn't been made to pay a cent. He was able to put all this in motion by filling out a five-page form. Government lawyers will do the rest.

Another example of the way homosexuals justify and rationalize their discriminatory hostility towards social conservatives comes to us from Provincetown, Massachusetts. Provincetown is apparently New England's "summer gay capital." But heterosexuals also live and vacation in the area. According to Reuters, this year "straight people" made complaints about being ridiculed by homosexuals with comments such as "breeders" and "baby makers." And an assault was reported in relation to a dispute over the definition of marriage.

"Police Chief Ted Meyer said straight people complained of being called 'breeders' over the July Fourth holiday weekend, and that in one serious incident a man was charged with assaulting a woman who signed a petition to ban same-sex marriage in Massachusetts, the only state where it is legal. Equally troubling, he said, Jamaican workers in Provincetown say they have been the target of racial slurs."[51]

51. "Gays accused of discrimination in resort village," by Jason Szep. Reuters, July 20, 2006.

What is even more troubling than the incidents themselves, however, is the rationalization of them by Joe Solmonese, the president of America's leading homosexual rights group, Human Rights Campaign: "Joe Solmonese… said the petition signers invited trouble by taking a position that says 'loud and clear that you believe that gays and lesbians should be treated as second class citizens'." Try remaining a free citizen if you took that position in an incident where the roles were reversed!

Hostility to Christianity in the public square, however, does not always come dressed in the clothes of a "barbarian." It is often sanitized, such as when it is advanced in sophisticated and respected segments of society. In academic circles, for example, the arguments that justify the persecution of Christians for the sake of justice and equality are already well developed.

In December 2005, the American Becket Fund for Religious Liberty sponsored a conference on religious freedom which brought together a significant number of lawyers and academics who have a reputation for expertise in this field. Conservative writer and analyst Maggie Gallagher wrote an extensive article in *The Weekly Standard*[52] on the outcome of that conference, and what she had to say predicts darkening storm clouds over America in coming years as a result of the ongoing battle between Christian faith and homosexual secularism, especially if marriage is redefined to include same-sex arrangements.

http://news.yahoo.com/s/nm/20060720/us_nm/rights_gays_dc.
52. "Banned in Boston: The coming conflict between same-sex marriage and religious liberty," by Maggie Gallagher. *Weekly Standard*, May 15, 2006, Volume 011, Issue 33. http://www.weeklystandard.com/Content/Public/Articles/000/000/012/191kgwgh. asp?pg=1.

The conference brought together people on both sides of the homosexual "marriage" controversy, including numerous highly respected legal experts. Many of them are convinced that there will be real clashes between the homosexual "marriage" agenda and religious liberty, although they did not agree on how serious those conflicts would be or how they might be resolved. Whatever else this says, it makes a mockery of the fraudulent claims by today's secular establishment that they represent the voice of tolerance and accommodation.

Marc Stern, who has handled religious freedom cases for the American Jewish Congress for many years and is considered an expert in this field, says he firmly believes that legal recognition of same-sex marriage will make clashes with religious liberty "inevitable." In fact, he anticipates that the conflict is "going to be a train wreck"—one that he believes can be avoided only if advocates on both sides renounce what he called "a winner take all" attitude.

"No one seriously believes that clergy will be forced, or even asked, to perform marriages that are anathema to them," Mr. Stern has written. But for Christians in other circumstances, he believes legal acceptance of homosexual "marriage" would have a "substantial impact." "He has in mind schools, health care centers, social service agencies, summer camps, homeless shelters, nursing homes, orphanages, retreat houses, community centers, athletic programs and private businesses or services that operate by religious standards, like kosher caterers and marriage counselors," clarified the *New York Times*.[53]

Considering the state of anti-Christian sentiment even among scholars and academics, the immediate future does not look

53. "Will Same-Sex Marriage Collide With Religious Liberty?" by Peter Steinfels. *New York Times*, June 10, 2006. http://www.nytimes.com/2006/06/10/us/10beliefs.html.

good for social conservative Christians. Also speaking at the Becket Fund conference was Chai R. Feldblum, a professor at Georgetown University Law Center, who refers to herself as "part of an inner group of public-intellectual movement leaders committed to advancing LGBT [lesbian, gay, bisexual, transsexual] equality." She acknowledged that "we are in a zero-sum game in terms of moral values."[54] There will be an absolute loser and an absolute winner. And despite her recognition as a First Amendment scholar, she argued that exterminating religious liberty is a satisfactory price to pay for strengthening homosexual rights: "In her view, the dignity and equality of gay people should almost always outweigh considerations of religious freedom, though she believes that such freedom might weigh more heavily for religious institutions 'geared just towards members of the faith' as opposed to those that interact broadly with the general public."[55] How nice of her to give us that!

Will homosexual secular activists push too far? It is hard to say, but there was some minor evidence of backlash in Canada in 2006, following despicable behaviour by some homosexuals. In August, the *Montreal Gazette* even published a letter from a self-identified homosexual rightly labelling other homosexuals as fascists. He was responding to media reports that the audience at Montreal's homosexual "Outgames" booed the federal Cabinet Minister who went to address the crowd on behalf of the Prime Minister and the government of Canada.

"As someone who is 'out'," began the letter-writer, "I was outraged by the hypocritical conduct of tens of thousands people (sic) who booed Public Works Minister Michael Fortier

54. Ibid.
55. Ibid.

35

so intensely during his remarks at the opening ceremony of the Outgames that our mayor had to intervene to remind us 'this is Montreal' ... Like the neofascists that they supposedly despise, those who had denied free speech decided to carry on booing and ruin the show. This, sadly, is proof many thousands of Montrealers who happen to be gay and lesbian are as intolerant as the homophobes who have made many of our lives hell."[56]

Some journalists also condemned the "goon-squad" behaviour of these homosexuals, with the *Ottawa Citizen* titling Brigitte Pellerin's column, "When the tolerant behave like ignorant bigots."

> It's one thing to be sympathetic to, or at least tolerant of, a way of life that differs markedly from your own. It's quite another to be called names because you don't actively celebrate lifestyles that couldn't be more at odds with yours. I wish gay activists would understand the difference and leave the rest of us non-parade-goers alone.
>
> ... Troubles started on Friday, when singer k.d. lang slammed Prime Minister Stephen Harper for not planning to attend the event. "It's a sad statement that the national leader of a country that's one of the most progressive countries in the world chooses to support intolerance," she said during a news conference at Montreal's Olympic Stadium. "It's our job to see that as an unfortunate ignorance, rather than as a statement against us," she added, somewhat incongruously. "It's just that he hasn't got there in his heart"...

56. "Gay hypocrites," by G. DeWolf Shaw. *Montreal Gazette*, August 1, 2006

Sure, Mr. Harper is opposed to same-sex marriage. And yes, he promised during the campaign to debate the issue anew in the House of Commons. But opposing gay marriage does not necessarily mean being against homosexuals or even being homophobic, as the staggeringly obtuse and chronically offended among us seem to believe (funny how the people who talk our ears off about the need to be open-minded and nuanced can't seem to listen to or grasp the subtleties of ideas they don't share).[57]

It is essential for people to understand that it is not fringe lunatics within the homosexual movement who are behaving like this; it is leaders and figure-heads like singer k.d. lang who are fuelling this kind of uncivilised, bigoted behaviour. Both Ms. lang and former tennis star Martina Navratilova were highlighted by the media for their ignorant slurs. Outside the homosexual subculture, people like that would get their mouths washed out with soap (or would have had it done a few years back). What does it say about the homosexual movement that such people are, in fact, their heroes?

Also in July and August of 2006, a dispute arose among homosexuals over a despotic and insecure attempt by the Vancouver Pride Society to trademark the word "pride." "We just want to make sure the word isn't abused," was the juvenile defence for this move given by the society's vice-president, John Boychuck. "The move to trademark 'pride' was spearheaded by Pride Toronto, the largest Pride organization in Canada," reported the *Kingston Whig-Standard*.[58] Folding their comment on this controversy into a comment on the treatment of Prime Minister Stephen Harper at Montreal's

57. "When the tolerant behave like ignorant bigots," by Brigitte Pellerin. *The Ottawa Citizen*, August 1, 2006

"Outgames," the *Whig-Standard* observed: "Those athletes sounded a little close-minded themselves. Gay rights activists in Canada deserve much credit for strides they have made in lobbying legislators for stronger hate crimes laws, same-sex spousal benefits and same-sex marriage. And there is still much work to done in society to fight discrimination based on sexual orientation. But it's hard to be proud of organizations attempting to prevent others from essentially using a word that is already synonymous with the gay rights movement worldwide."

National Post columnist Colby Cosh importantly noted that Mr. Harper's attendance at the "Outgames" would probably have reasonably been considered a security risk: "It is doubtful, in fact, that a security apparatus with its head screwed on straight would have let him go near Montreal. Maybe it's fair for gays and lesbians to regard Harper as satanic for his opposition to gay marriage—but given his known policy preferences, why do they want him darkening the door of the Outgames at all?"[59]

There is growing evidence that humiliation, ostracism, monetary persecution and even physical harm should be treated as genuine concern by those openly critical of homosexuality. The militant assault against renowned ethicist Margaret Somerville in the summer of 2006 is a case study on the bigotry and raw hatred of some homosexual activists against even reasoned, science-backed, non-religious critics of homosexuality. Thankfully, with the intolerance in this case being so transparent, the extremists found many critics within the mainstream media. Unfortunately, however, as in the case of Islamo-fascist terrorists, those expecting condemnation

59. "Chariots of ire," By Colby Cosh. *National Post*, August 1, 2006.

58. "Prejudice or pride?," *Kingston Whig-Standard*, August 1, 2006.

from supposedly moderate, mainstream homosexuals were met instead with deafening silence.

Facing militant hostility from homosexual activists at her Ryerson University honorary degree ceremony, Ms. Somerville expressed shock. But what is really shocking is that she would be shocked. This is the kind of treatment Christians have experienced for years at the hands of homosexual activists. Sometimes they sanitize their hatred by channelling it through human rights commissions, but all this behaviour flows from hatred of dissent, intolerance toward disagreement and a generally totalitarian, censorship-advocating worldview.

The next question is: why is this mentality or perspective so entrenched within the homosexual political movement? The reason is straightforward: it is an expression of secularism. As we have already discussed, secularism is totalitarian in nature. It is socialism; an ideology of political centralism. It is a religion in which the state is god. And this weak and decrepit god, as in the case of all false gods, cannot tolerate dissent.

The reason why this militant totalitarian mentality is more transparently expressed by homosexual activists than other secularists is probably due to the sexual nature of the homosexual agenda. Sexuality is perhaps the most intense passion people experience. Is this not why a culture with a growing number of people unable and unwilling to control their sexual passions starts to push for the elimination of laws against the perverse expressions of this passion? In order to deal with their guilty consciences, they have to redefine morality and treat these perverse sexual expressions as normal, and if they are normal, how can we have laws against them?

Sexual passion is intense. Unrestrained perverse sexual passion is even more intense. If someone consumed by sexual passion thinks he is going to be restrained, he must imagine the only outcome for himself as being insanity. Would he not feel like a cornered animal? Unrestrained sexual passion enslaves people. It makes people ripe for control and manipulation. This is why homosexuals make excellent front-line warriors for secularist ideologues who want to exploit them to advance their own revolutionary agenda on Canada.

Many homosexuals know that they are enslaved and many would love to be rescued if they had the support system necessary to give them the courage to try to escape. But activists need these foot-soldiers, so they militantly deny that homosexuality is something that people can be delivered from. Instead of offering deliverance to those who want to be rescued, they seek to keep them in bondage. These ideologues are the ones who truly hate other homosexuals. They are simply exploiting them for an ideological agenda.[60]

Evidence of the Secularist establishment's exploitation of homosexuality is the fact that public debate surrounding homosexuality is dominated extensively by "human rights" arguments instead of medical and health issues. In fact, the re very serious health implications of homosexuality are played down in many cases. A recent report in the *New York Times* discusses the prevalence of anal cancer among

---

60. "Why Gays Can Not Be 'Pro-Choice'," by Kevin McCullough. November 26, 2006. http://www.townhall.com/Columnists/KevinMcCullough/2006/11/26/why_gays_can_not_be_pro-choice. In contrast, Christians need to increase the profile of their message of deliverance for homosexuals from sexual bondage. This is a message of genuine grace and charity, and is the constructive counter to the hate-based homosexual agenda of Secular Humanism. Ex-homosexual Stephen Bennett has an excellent ministry <http://www.sbministries.org/> in this regard, as does Focus on the Family with their Love Won Out <http://www.lovewonout.com/> seminars.

homosexuals.[61] The article noted that HPV, the most common sexually transmitted infection in the U.S. is the source of anal cancer. Yet, in what is a common refrain for homosexuals wracked with disease, the article reported that "many gay men do not realize they have an elevated risk of anal cancer." A San Francisco resident was quoted: "I had no idea about [the risk of anal cancer] because no one ever talked about it, although these days more gay men seem to be aware of it." More people don't hear about homosexuality-related diseases because it isn't to the advantage of Secular Humanists to publicize these medical facts. The indiscriminate affirmation of homosexuality, which is the message conveyed by Canada's Secularist politicians, academics and mainstream media outlets, clearly does not reflect a commitment of dignity or charity towards homosexuals.

What is a religion?

A key deception in the claims of Secular Humanism is the labelling of Christianity and other "traditional" religions as "religions," while claiming that Secularism is not a religion. Too many Christians talk as though they have also accepted this notion. One sees something of this assumption in a May 2005 column in *The Georgia Straight*, Vancouver's lifestyle and entertainment weekly. In the article, author Shannon Rupp writes: "Because the Secular society respects all outlooks but doesn't advocate any of them, something like the Christian creationist myth couldn't be taught as fact in science classes at the public schools."[62]

61. "New Vaccine for Cervical Cancer Could Prove Useful in Men, Too," by David Tuller. *The New York Times*, January 30, 2007.
62. "The return of God," by Shannon Rupp. *The Georgia Straight*, May 19, 2005.

The relevant point here is not the teaching of creationism, but how the author describes "Secular society." In the preceding paragraph of her article, Ms. Rupp indicated her belief that "Secular" is synonymous with "liberal." Identifying confusion over the meaning of "Secular," she allows John Russell, a political-philosophy instructor at Langara College and a former president of the B.C. Civil Liberties Association, to provide the definition: "Russell provides an accurate description: 'A liberal society is neutral; it maintains the dignity of all. It provides the means for living the good life but it doesn't promote specific ways of life. So it ensures equal rights to liberty, due process in law, security of person—but none of these things defines a Secular or a religious approach to life'."[63]

There are numerous errors in Mr. Russell's proposition, not least being the fact that he burgles Christianity of principles that flow directly out of a Judaeo-Christian worldview and attributes them to Secularism, which he inaccurately labels "liberalism." Secularism is the antithesis of the neutral, passive, liberty-enhancing model that Mr. Russell claims. Rather, it is a ruthlessly oppressive regime that is committed to a winner-takes-all war against Christianity. If Secularism defeats Christianity, it will also rob Canadian civilization of the legal, social and political principles that flow from a Christian worldview, such as equal rights to liberty, due process in law and security of the person, just as it has in every other country that has experimented with socialism, communism and fascism. Notwithstanding the definition proposed by Mr. Russell, Secularism does not provide us with a political realm that is value-neutral, where people holding competing views can meet to dialogue and find consensus.

63. Ibid.

But what of the claim that it is not a religion? What is religion? What does it mean to be religious? These questions could be considered and addressed from various perspectives. For the purposes of the topic at hand, we need to understand Christianity as a worldview. This means that whatever else Christianity is, it is a body of law, moral direction, knowledge and truth that gives meaning to life and that governs every area of life. In other words, people who want to call themselves Christians can be confident that the Christian roadmap—the Bible—gives them all the direction they need to live the life that the God they worship demands of them. For the purpose of legitimate comparison, Judaism, Islam and Hinduism are also worldviews. They have their own source of professed truth and law, which is designed to give their adherents the moral direction they need for life.

What is different, in this respect, for Secular Humanists, atheists, agnostics or anyone else who claims to be irreligious? Nothing. Even for people who claim to draw their beliefs about right and wrong from inside themselves, they still draw them from somewhere. They do not live in a moral or intellectual vacuum. All people develop a moral code from somewhere. It might be Charles Darwin's racist and eugenic "survival of the fittest" philosophy or Karl Marx's ruthless *Communist Manifesto*, or perhaps it is an incoherent amalgamation of several incompatible worldviews, such as one might get from watching any selection of five or six of the most popular of today's TV shows. The point is that for the purposes of political discourse, in terms of philosophical categories, Secularism is comparable with Christianity and other worldviews. It is only by way of the arrogant and false "faith vs. reason" construct that Secularists can attempt to marginalize Christianity as an inferior worldview to their own—and, therefore, innately less deserving of playing a role in the civil governance of a nation.

Notably, when David Rudenstine gave his June 2005 address and was asked, "Isn't extreme Secularism a faith itself," he "did not respond."[64]

Secularists also get away with their caricature of Christianity because of the constant, self-marginalizing use of the same language by Christians. It was particularly evident in the recent battle over the definition of marriage: Christians constantly appealed to their freedom of religion or their "religiously informed" conscience[65] as the basis for their right to hold views on marriage deemed discriminatory by the Secular political establishment.

As part of a broader message, that is fine, but standing alone, as that declaration often was, it is not only self-marginalizing language, it is also un-Christian because it shows Christians as only interested in protecting their own self-interest. It is language that does not protect the free speech and freedom of conscience rights of those who oppose homosexual "marriage" for sociological and scientific reasons. It only protects those who claim a "religious" foundation for their views.

Christian author and singer Pat Boone contrasts the comprehensive vision of liberty for all that is rooted in

64. "Collision Course; Secular Justifications; New Religious Schools; 'Reasonable Faith'," by Thomas Adcock. *The New York Law Journal*, June 17, 2005, p. 16.
65. E.g., "Same sex marriage is contrary to my personal beliefs and to my religious faith," MP Guy Lauzon (Stormont—Dundas—South Glengarry, CPC), House of Commons, April 5, 2005. "Todd, like millions of Americans, obviously has a moral conviction based on his **religious** beliefs against homosexual behavior and that lifestyle. There is absolutely nothing wrong with that," (emphasis added), American Family Association as cited in "Christian landscaper won't soil hands with work for 'gay' clients," WorldNetDaily.com, October 21, 2006, http://worldnetdaily.com/news/article.asp?ARTICLE_ID=52554.

Christianity with the sectarian oppressiveness of the Secular Humanist ACLU. "Compare the concept of democracy— where individuals may speak and act and express their faith according to their own understanding—with theocracy, where an elite few dictate what all individuals can and cannot say, do or express concerning their beliefs,"[66] he wrote. "Now think ACLU."

He continued:

> "Think an elitist coterie who twist and redefine the expressed intentions of the framers of the Constitution in order to defend anarchists, pedophiles, sworn enemies of our nation, aberrant sexual practices, blasphemies of all kinds and attacks on our hallowed institutions – and who at the same time proceed against every kind of public expression of faith or religion, always misappropriating a phrase not even in our Constitution, "separation of church and state"…

> Think *theocratic dictatorship*. "Wait," you may say, "theocracy denotes religion. The ACLU is opposed to religion and religious expression! How can they be associated with theocracy?" I'll tell you…. On CNN's Crossfire… I said. "Michael [Newdow],[67] you know that your atheism is a religion; it's a faith system on which you stake your life, based on the premise that God doesn't exist—a premise you can't prove. Our faith is based on the premise that God *does* exist, and the evidence is literally everywhere. You know

66. "The ACLU: A bunch of theocrats?," by Pat Boone. WorldNetDaily (September 2, 2006). http://www.worldnetdaily.com/news/article.asp?ARTICLE_ID=51793.
67. Michael NewDow is the American atheist activist who is constantly in court trying to get "under God" deleted from the American Pledge of Allegiance.

that atheism is in itself a religion, don't you?" A*nd he agreed it is!...* I call [his activism] an attempt to establish one concept of religion over all others and to silence any alternatives.

CHAPTER TWO

SECULARISM:
HYPOCRISY AS RELIGION

Secularism is inherently state-ist

The best way to understand a religion is to know who or what is worshiped; what is deemed absolute. Secularism is inherently state-ist. State-ism is the worship of the civil government. Secularists, as socialists, advocate the absolute power of the state (although most of them today are far too subtle to say so forthrightly). The civil magistrate is deemed the arbiter of human rights and justice—and not just any part of the civil government: we are talking specifically about the aristocratic elite of the "judge-ocracy," as opposed to the elected representatives of the people. And not just any level of government; rather the federal government—and one day, they hope, the ultimate in centralized, absolute authority, a comprehensive international political order—one-world government. This is also why Secularists have to subjugate the church and the family under the state, increasingly eliminating any independent authority exercised by these institutions.

As you can see, Secularists are not just religious, they are religious "fanatics"—philosophically consistent, pedantic purists.[1]

For Secularists, the state embodies many characteristics that Christians attribute to God, including final authority, centralized power, omniscience (the ability to know all things), or at least the possession of sufficient knowledge to give the state superior decision-making skills in terms of such fundamental issues as health care and child care.

American author and commentator Ann Coulter summarizes the Secularist faith succinctly in her latest book, *Godless: The Church of Liberalism*.[2] "Abortion is the sacrament and *Roe v. Wade* is holy writ." As an example of a liberal, or secular, saint, she identifies former president John F. Kennedy. One of Liberalism's martyrs was Soviet spy Alger Hiss. Their clergy include public school teachers and the media. Their churches are government monopoly schools where expressions of Christianity including prayer are being progressively banned. Their anthropology identifies man as an accident and their cosmology and "Creation myth" is Darwinian evolution, the

1. French historian Alexis de Tocqueville was perhaps a little more refined in the way he discussed the religious nature of liberal democrats, the precursors of today's secularists. John von Heyking, Associate Professor of Political Science at University of Lethbridge, discussed Tocqueville's observations at a June 2006 Centre for Cultural Renewal conference on the Cooperation of Church & State. "Democracy makes its own faith-claims. ... Faith in 'progress,' in a future that is ever more perfect than what has come before, is just as much based on an act of faith [as] faith in the death and resurrection of Christ because it postulates a perfect utopian society—a democratic utopia—that our current elites are supposedly bringing about. ... So, for Tocqueville, liberal democrats are characterized by a tendency to place their faith in a utopian hope for a society based on perfect equality and individual self-realization and creativity. Christians can do something to moderate that utopianism by advancing their own ideas of political society."

2. *Godless: The Church of Liberalism* by Ann Coulter. Publisher: Crown Forum, June 6, 2006. 384 pages. ISBN: 140054206.

protected status of which is constantly defended with lawsuits to censor all competing theories.

Pioneering Canadian Conservative columnist Ted Byfield, who often rails against the activist nature of today's courts, makes the point cogently:

> Whether ancient or modern, every human society, it seems, must have a priesthood, a cast of men or women upon whom is conferred a final, absolute, virtually infallible authority, particularly as regards morality and the law. It's essential for the credibility of this authority that it be duly and publicly respected, honoured, esteemed, even venerated. Those who belong to it must not be viewed as ordinary people. They must be seen as of a higher, nobler, more august order of humanity. Otherwise, of course, the commoners may begin to challenge their authority, to doubt their pontifications, to question that which must never be doubted.
>
> In our society, going back some 800 years, that authority was vested in the clergy.... we in Canada are about to take the next step... in favour of a new priesthood, the priesthood of the judges. They are our new rulers and already they are working to endow their office with due nobility and divine decorum as the new magisterium. "Canadians appear to share a profound belief that when other institutions fail, one can count on the fairness of the courts," says one jurist who notes a "radical alteration in the public perception of judges"... These words are those of Chief Justice Beverley McLachlin...

There were a couple of points about this new role for judges that the chief justice didn't get around to mentioning. Point 1: The Canadian Supreme Court has taken upon itself the job of making laws... Point 3: This makes us what amounts to an authoritarian state. We are no longer a democracy.[3]

Mr. Byfield also made some important points about the judges of the Supreme Court of Canada's god-like powers in response to the short-lived firestorm in May, 2006 surrounding Conservative MP Maurice Vellacott's comments criticizing judicial activism.[4]

Now if any institution should properly speak out in protest against this particular outrage, surely it is Parliament itself, the body whose centuries-old powers are being blithely pirated by a Supreme Court-gone-nuts, drunk with delusions of an unlimited mandate to exercise supra-parliamentary authority.

[Mr. Vellacott's] offence was to criticize Chief Justice Beverley McLachlin's notably exalted description of a judge's role, delivered in her celebrated speech in New Zealand.[5] She said, Vellacott charged, that when lawyers become judges, "all of a sudden there's some mystical kind of power comes over them by which everything that they ever decree then is not to be questioned, they take on these almost godlike powers." Well, the chief justice admittedly did not use those precise

3. *Judges form Canada's 'new priesthood'*, by Ted Byfield. April 4, 2004
4. *Do not go beating up on the 'god-like'*, by Ted Byfield. *Calgary Sun*, May 21, 2006. http://calsun.canoe.ca/News/Columnists/Byfield_Ted/2006/05/21/1590636.html.
5. *Unwritten Constitutional Principles: What is Going On?*, by Chief Justice Beverely McLachlin, Supreme Court of Canada. 2005 Lord Cooke Lecture, Wellington, New Zealand, December 1, 2005.

words. But careful examination of the powers of moral perception which she did attribute to judges confirms that something very like it is certainly implied. Unless judges have been somehow endowed with the power to discern and invent "new natural law," as she calls it, whereas mere elected politicians lack that power, then how could the court justify making up laws, rather than allowing Parliament to do it? There's only one possible answer: judges have mystical qualifications not bestowed upon most mortals. If that indeed is what she is asserting, Vellacott is right....

Contrast, for example, these two views of the function of a judge:

First, the McLachlin view as delivered in New Zealand: "There exist fundamental norms of justice so basic they form part of the legal structure of governance and must be upheld by the courts, whether or not they find expression in constitutional texts."

Second, a very different view: "Canada is a federation in which Parliament and the provincial legislatures make the laws. When Parliament or the legislatures have conferred a discretionary power on judges, that discretion must be exercised within the bounds established by the legislatures or Parliament."

By the first view, judges are at liberty to ignore restraints imposed by "constitutional texts," meaning the Charter and the laws passed by federal Parliament and provincial legislatures. By the second view, judges are to act "within the bounds established by the legislatures

and Parliament." Thus judges are not above the written laws. They are, in effect, not "like gods."[6]

Constitutional attorney and founder and president of The Rutherford Institute, John W. Whitehead, makes the point about the state-ist nature of Secularism by contrasting the pro-family commitment of Christianity with the implications of family breakdown, embraced, as it has been, by Secularism.

Third, the data [on the breakdown of the American family] supports the premise that the decline in the family leads to a decline in our democracy. Indeed, the family is where children should learn self-government, basic moral values and the beliefs that determine the future of democratic institutions. Thus, it stands to

6. For further evidence of Secular Humanism's use of the state to clamp down on Christian liberty, Rory Leishman's new book, "Against Judicial Activism: The Decline of Freedom and Democracy in Canada" [Publisher: McGill-Queen's University Press, May 1, 2006. 310 pages. ISBN-10: 0773530541.], is a must-read. Reviewing the book, Ray Pennings of the Work Research Foundation ("Two minutes for elbowing: Competing for influence and cultural change," by Ray Pennings. Comment, August 2006), observes, "Leishman suggests the pattern is not entirely random. His book is filled with the chronology of cases which have effectively changed the law in the contentious fields of education and social policy. The absence of any abortion law in Canada, the militant secular agenda, and the redefini-tion of marriage to incorporate same-sex marriage have their roots in court decisions.... Leishman recounts how courts have interpreted 'current notions of justice and fairness' to exclude expressions of religiously inspired notions of justice and fairness in the public square. In the Surrey School Board case, a decision against including books favourably depicting same-sex parents in the kindergarten curriculum was overturned by the courts on the grounds that trustees were influenced by the religious convictions: 'I conclude that the words "conducted on strictly secular principles" (words that are included in the British Columbia School Act which the judge was interpreting) precludes a decision significantly influenced by religious considerations' notes the decision of the local judge, ultimately up-held by the Supreme Court (169-176)... In Leishman's view, the evidence is clear. Not only are the courts misusing their authority creating legal chaos, they are advancing a specific agenda, one that is creating a climate in which religious freedom is being curtailed. With an approving quote from Professor Ian Hunter, Leishman concludes his chapter: 'The Supreme Court has ruled there is a right to believe what you want as long as you never communicate those beliefs or put them into practice. You are free to be hearers of the The Word but not doers; You may render unto God when [in church] but only to Caesar [out of church]. By their deeds no one shall know them' (194)."

reason that without stable families, we can have no hope of producing self-reliant, responsible citizens.

Fourth, the increasing loss of the family structure leads to destabilization in society of "mediating structures"— neighborhoods, families, churches, schools and voluntary associations. When they function as they should, mediating structures limit the growth of the government. But when these structures break down, society—that is, people—look to mega-structures, such as the state, as a source of values. In America, the state-financed public schools and day care centers have increasingly assumed the role of providing "values" for children. As history teaches, the authoritarian state gladly and aggressively assumes this role and becomes a substitute family.

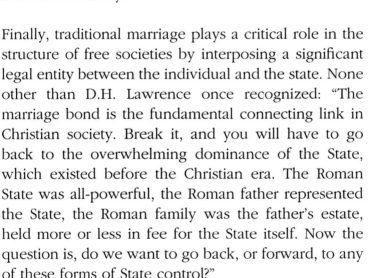

Finally, traditional marriage plays a critical role in the structure of free societies by interposing a significant legal entity between the individual and the state. None other than D.H. Lawrence once recognized: "The marriage bond is the fundamental connecting link in Christian society. Break it, and you will have to go back to the overwhelming dominance of the State, which existed before the Christian era. The Roman State was all-powerful, the Roman father represented the State, the Roman family was the father's estate, held more or less in fee for the State itself. Now the question is, do we want to go back, or forward, to any of these forms of State control?"

Lawrence continued: "It is marriage, perhaps, which has given man the best of his freedom, given him his little kingdom of his own within the big kingdom of the State, given him his foothold of independence on which to stand and resist an unjust State. Man and wife, a king and queen with one or two subjects, and a few square yards of territory of their own: this, really, is marriage. It is a true freedom because it is a true fulfillment, for man, woman, and children."[7]

The state is god for the Secular Humanist, even if he chooses not to use such terminology.[8] Secularists, of course, do not accept this analysis. It is not to their advantage to do so. But it is the only valid analysis.

U.S. Catholic statesman, and former presidential candidate, Alan Keyes, identifies clearly the relationship between belief in God and the practise of self-government over against Secular Humanism's worship of the civil government—and the Total War agenda of Secularism against the foundation of civil-social liberty. "If you assail the right of the people to honor God, then you assail the first principle of their self-government, which is that we are endowed by our Creator with unalienable rights leading to the consequence that the only form of government that is legitimate is a form of government that respects those God-given rights. No God, no republic. No God, no representation. No God, no due process. No God, no sanctity of individual rights, liberty, and life. The denial of God is an assault not only upon the people's conscience, but upon their claim to have from God the right to govern themselves through representative institutions.

7. "Without the Family, There Is No Freedom", by John W. Whitehead. *The Rutherford Institute*, December 28, 2006.

8. Chapter 5 goes into much more detail about the religious nature of Secularism. At that stage, we also discuss Secularism's kinship with German Nazism which, in most circles, has been fraudulently labelled a right-wing phenomenon. *The Libertarian Ludwig von Mises Institute* published an excellent article by George Reisman, Ph.D., explaining this point as their November 11, 2005 *Mises Daily Article*. It was called, "Why Nazism was Socialism and Why Socialism is Totalitarian."

The triumph of this false doctrine of separation, therefore, portends not only the persecution of our faith, but the destruction of our liberty."[9]

Religion and rationality

Having labelled Christianity as a "blind faith" religion (as contrasted with supposedly "reasoned" Secularism), Secularists have been able to get away with other logical fallacies and irrational rhetorical flourishes to further marginalize Christians and the Christian position on controversial issues.

Using the reference to Christianity as a religion, they maintain, for example, that the Christian position on abortion is a religious position in contrast to their supposedly scientific Secularist position. This does not constitute a legitimate argument. It is an attempt to demonize the Christian position so as to deflect any attempt to be forced to present an intellectual case that is logically consistent with Secularist presuppositions. For example, Secularists say that the pro-life position in general is a religious position whereas a pro-choice position is not. This is a logical fallacy. One can approach the matter of abortion from different vantage points: theological, philosophical, medical, biological, etc. If one approaches it from a biological perspective, then as long as both sides are faithful to the terms of reference for a biological discussion, then both competing positions would properly be classified as biological in nature. To claim, on the other hand, that a pro-life position is religious in nature simply because it is pro-life, regardless of how that position is presented, is a logical fallacy, and probably the most extreme example of intellectual dishonesty in public discourse today.

9. *Patriot Post*, Vol. 07 No. 03, January 15, 2007.

If Christians would cultivate the kind of intellectual rigor that is consistent with the standard of excellence that God demands in every area of life, they would not be put on the defensive by such foolish, disrespectful and intellectually embarrassing attacks. Unfortunately, due to Secularists' success at marginalizing that which they condescendingly refer to as religious and, therefore, anti-rational, they maintain this fundamentally dishonest paradigm which sets them apart from religion. This paradigm also, therefore, presents Secularists as the primary, if not exclusive, possessors of reason (and hence, as we shall see, of open-mindedness, moderation and tolerance).

Where is the realm of moral neutrality?

Regretfully, many Christians have joined others in accepting the notion that there exists a neutral meeting ground where fair-minded adherents of any and all worldviews or belief systems can iron out their differences and achieve compromises that are palatable to all. This Secularist notion is simply a perverse distortion of natural law theory, which already (in its supposedly Christian form) has its own set of problems.

Contrary to that view, fundamental to the notion of a worldview is that it proposes public as well as private values. That is, a worldview addresses public, corporate life. It deals with what is acceptable behaviour, and what is unacceptable, when it comes to economic relations, civil law, social order and public policy. A worldview does not simply deal with the realm of so-called private morality. Hence, when a Christian puts forth a Christian position on public policy and a Muslim proposes something else, and they find a "compromise," that compromise is no longer the Christian position and it is probably not the Muslim position either. To demand that such compromises be the method for establishing law and public policy is to demand that Christians deny fundamental elements of their Christian worldview. The same is the case for Muslims, Buddhists, Jews and just about everyone else. (If a Muslim compromised with Jews or Christians for the sake of political theory, then the final result would not be faithful to Islam.) Whatever this approach to public policy might be, it is incompatible with any coherent notion of a God who claims Lordship and sovereignty over all of life, including the sphere of civil governance.[10]

Moral neutrality and theological equivalence reflect a mentality of defeat. That is the historic record and the prophetic assurance from God.[11] The type of compromise demanded by Secularism is not compatible with a Christian ethic of leadership.

For an outsider to tell someone of another faith—the way Secular Humanists do of Christians—that he can be faithful to his own faith without advocating its demands on public morality is the height of arrogance. Such an attitude is one of tyranny and oppression, and that is the nature of Secular Humanism.

10. This mentality of compromise is a key factor in the problem that most Americans and Europeans have with finding the intellectual terms of reference necessary for understanding the non-compromising approach to law and civil governance advanced today by Islam. This approach to compromise probably shares the same theological foundation as the accommodationist approach that most Western leaders took towards communism after World War II until Ronald Reagan became President of the United States. Reagan, with the help of British Prime Minister Margaret Thatcher and Pope John Paul II, snatched victory out of the hands of an ideological commitment to defeat, a commitment that even seemed to be shared by a large segment of the Western church of the day.

11. "He who is not with Me is against Me," Matthew 12:30 (North American Standard Bible); Samuel to King Saul: "For rebellion is as the sin of divination, and insubordination is as iniquity and idolatry. Because you have rejected the word of the LORD, He has also rejected you from being king," I Samuel 15:23).

Listen to the arrogance and self-righteousness of a homosexual activist defending the participation of socialist Catholic MP Joe Comartin (NDP—Windsor-Tecumseh, ON) in a "Gay Pride" parade—as the parade's official marshal, no less: "The diocese reaction had better be very minimal," said [former priest Joe] McParland, the Windsor Pride board president. "The diocese and the church are not in a position to censure people's freedom of action and gathering. Joe is now strictly in the arena of politics. It has nothing to do with his expression of faith. It is a political statement, not a faith statement."[12]

Another example of this arrogance is found in the May 2005 media feeding frenzy against Christians due to the fact that Christians won some Conservative Party nominations leading up to the 2006 election—and won these nominations in urban areas and in Atlantic Canada. One publication wrote: "The CPC has nominated fundamentalist Christians for a number of ridings. Not that there's anything wrong with religion, but religion and politics should not be mixed. Whatever an individual politician or candidate believes in is really his or her own private business, but the problem here is that these nominees have come out and stated that they will no longer be ashamed of who they are and that they will pursue their political goals guided by their religious beliefs."[13] Why does this Secular Humanist writer assert that Christians have no right living as Christians when they step outside the four walls of their home and church? His position is not rooted in an intellectually defensible argument. More likely, his position is a rhetorical offensive against the kind of public policy positions he expects a Christian politician to hold and advance.

12. "Comartin to lead Pride ride: MP, police chief, mayor join parade for first time," by Trevor Wilhelm. *The Windsor Star*, July 14, 2006.
13. Cf. "Witch Hunt: Burn the Christians," Bound by Gravity blog, May 28, 2005, http://www.boundbygravity.com/archives/2005/05/witch_hunt_burn_the_christians.php.

We need to understand that Secular Humanism is not the realm of moral neutrality. No worldview is morally neutral. Secular Humanism is a worldview with its own set of distinct moral demands—demands which require singular devotion to Secular Humanism at the expense of competing faiths or worldviews. Secular Humanists proselytize as militantly as the most aggressive evangelists of other faiths, and due to the ruthless and tyrannical nature of Secular Humanism, the intimidating ideology is swiftly gaining influence by scaring people into compliance, regardless of whether or not such people become personal devotees of the Secular Humanist religion. Secular Humanism is a jealous religion, and will not share its place of primacy in a person's life with any other worldview that makes absolute and competing claims for truth and morality. Secularism is one of the most intolerant, uncompromising ideologies invented by man.

Christians cannot be faithful to their faith or to the God of their faith if they compromise with Secular Humanism and its demands. Christians must argue—and have a right to argue— on behalf of their own worldview and attempt, through just means, to influence the law, public affairs and social order in their country. Everyone who genuinely believes in his worldview believes it is the best way to live and think, so he wants to see others adopt his views, and he wants his worldview to become increasingly influential in the affairs of men. Hence, if Christianity is not the driving force behind the laws and public policy in Canada, another religion or worldview will be. Whenever this appears not to be the case (when compromise looks like it is working), it is only because the civilization is in a state of transition from the dominance of one worldview to the control of another.

It is remarkable, the number of Christians who argue against the applicability of Christian truth to law and public policy, or at least who argue against the exclusive application of Christianity to law and public policy. Such a stance is not rational and it reinforces the stereotypes that Secularists have of Christianity. A case in point is Randall Balmer, professor of religion at Barnard College in New York and editor-at-large of the Evangelical magazine *Christianity Today*. He has recently published a book—*Thy Kingdom Come: An Evangelical's Lament*[14]—condemning Evangelical conservative political activism. As a professed Evangelical, he claims to write as an insider, a perception the liberal media is only too happy to promote.

Despite being a professor of religion and recognized as a historian, Mr. Balmer's grasp of both history and Evangelical theology are embarrassingly bizarre. A review in the Roman Catholic journal, *First Things*, charges that:

> *"Thy Kingdom Come"*... is indistinguishable from the general run of secularist hysterics, save for a smug reference to Balmer's spotless Sunday school attendance record and a patina of "real Baptist" outrage over how the Religious Right has supposedly hijacked his heritage.... There's certainly room, after thirty years of culture war, for an informed and evenhanded critique of Christian conservatism, and Balmer's background would seem to make him an ideal writer for the job. But while he occasionally nods in the direction of intelligent criticism—noting the disparity between the Christian Right's fixation on gay marriage, say, and its

---

14. *Thy Kingdom Come: How the Religious Right Distorts the Faith and Threatens America: An Evangelical's Lament*, by Randall Balmer. Publisher: Basic Books, July 3, 2006. 242 pages. ISBN: 0465005195.

long-running silence on divorce; or zinging religious conservatives for writing the Bush administration a blank check in the war on terror—these arguments are quickly dropped in favor of the usual litany of anti-theocrat complaints, flavored with the usual apocalyptic rhetoric.[15]

Judging by several reviews of his book,[16] Mr. Balmer thinks he has scored a great coup by revealing that the issue which apparently galvanized Evangelical political activism was the defence of religious liberty in the context of a battle over Bob Jones University's segregationist policies. The U.S. government wanted to rescind the Christian university's tax exempt status over these policies. Although the issue in question may not be particularly palatable, the principle that was being defended in this case was that of the separation of church and state. But, of course, throw the issue of race into a situation and few people, especially liberals, are able to continue to think straight. The point Mr. Balmer was making was that most Evangelicals think that their activism was founded in opposition to abortion, a more noble cause than apparently defending racism.

Mr. Balmer would have done himself and Evangelicals a much greater service if, instead, he praised this early work in defence of the separation of church and state. After all, one of his dominant themes is criticism against what he sees as the Evangelical-dominated social conservative movement's opposition to the separation of church and state. But, as with

15. "Theocracy, Theocracy, Theocracy," by Ross Douthat. *First Things*, August/September 2006. http://www.firstthings.com/ftissues/ft0607/articles/douthat.html.
16. "Current disputes revive question: What is an evangelical?," by Richard N. Ostling, *Associated Press*. "Still waiting for the great leap backward," by Brian Bethune. *New Brunswick Telegraph-Journal*, August 11, 2006. "Theocracy, Theocracy, Theocracy," by Ross Douthat. *Maclean's*, August 28, 2006. *First Things*, August/September 2006. http://www.firstthings.com/ftissues/ft0607/articles/douthat.html.

most people, he confuses separation of church and state with separation of religion from politics, and demonstrates that he un-Christianly supports the latter. He thinks he is advocating the separation of church and state, yet he condemns the early work of politically active Evangelicals for advancing just that principle. That is the kind of scholarship you can expect from this book.

Mr. Balmer is a stereotypical liberal, criticizing what he claims are Christian people working too closely with the civil governors, thus supposedly confusing the lines between church and state, and a religion that wants to be mainstream rather than on the fringes of society. Apparently Christians— conservative Christians anyway—in positions of political power resemble a movement that he does not recognize as Christian. But, buying into stale Secularist dogma, he even opposes work to advance academic choice, academic liberty and scientific investigation by condemning attempts to get "intelligent design" discussed in science courses, calling such pursuits "insidious." He opposes home schooling and vouchers that enhance choice in education and claims that the campaign to allow voluntary prayer in public schools is an attempt "to dismantle the First Amendment."

Mr. Balmer raises the spectre of theocracy as the goal of the Christian Right, pathetically insinuating that attempts to reintroduce Christian principles into civil government are inherently theocratic in nature and, as such, are anti-democratic. Firstly, that dichotomy is false. Secondly, theocracy has little meaning of value or interest outside of Presbyterian and Reformed circles, yet Presbyterian and Reformed Christians make up a minority of social conservative activists these days, so accusing the Christian Right of theocracy demonstrates theological illiteracy. Thirdly, his theological illiteracy and bias is evident in his lack of equal concern for the "theocratic" rule of Secularism.

The fact that many Christians feel more comfortable compromising with the application of non-Christian morality to law and public policy than they do with presenting a strong case for the moral superiority of Christianity is very disturbing. It would appear that at some subconscious level, many Christians have bought into the notion of their enemies that Christianity alone when applied to the civil governance of the nation is an expression of intolerance and fertile ground for destructive abuses—as though this risk factor sets Christianity apart from competing alternatives. But what Christians have to understand is that if Christianity is not good enough or comprehensive enough to be relevant in the realm of law and public policy, then Christianity is nothing more than a quaint intellectual novelty, a security blanket, a life-insurance policy coupled to an effective character development program.

We need to hear the words of columnist Paul Craig Roberts, who, in a column on Christmas, wrote about the importance of Christianity alone in incorporating the principles of human dignity and equality into the cultural and political system of the West.

> The decorations and gifts of Christmas are one of our connections to a Christian culture that has held Western civilization together for 2,000 years.
>
> In our culture, the individual counts. This permits an individual person to put his or her foot down, to take a stand on principle, to become a reformer and to take on injustice.

This empowerment of the individual is unique to Western civilization. It has made the individual a citizen equal in rights to all other citizens, protected from tyrannical government by the rule of law and free speech. These achievements are the products of centuries of struggle, but they all flow from the teaching that God so values the individual's soul that he sent his Son to die so we might live. By so elevating the individual, Christianity gave him a voice.

Formerly, only those with power had a voice. But in Western civilization, people with integrity have a voice. So do people with a sense of justice, of honor, of duty, of fair play. Reformers can reform, investors can invest, and entrepreneurs can create commercial enterprises, new products and new occupations. The result was a land of opportunity...

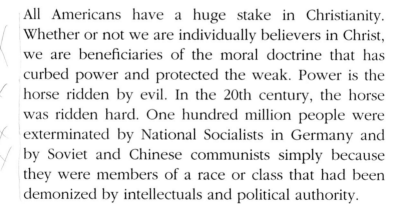

All Americans have a huge stake in Christianity. Whether or not we are individually believers in Christ, we are beneficiaries of the moral doctrine that has curbed power and protected the weak. Power is the horse ridden by evil. In the 20th century, the horse was ridden hard. One hundred million people were exterminated by National Socialists in Germany and by Soviet and Chinese communists simply because they were members of a race or class that had been demonized by intellectuals and political authority.

Power that is secularized and cut free of civilizing traditions is not limited by moral and religious scruples. V.I. Lenin made this clear when he defined the meaning of his dictatorship as "unlimited power, resting directly on force, not limited by anything."

> Christianity's emphasis on the worth of the individual
> makes such power as Lenin claimed unthinkable.[17]

Regretfully, too many of today's Christians are unaware of this Christian impact on culture and political theory—let alone the fact that this contribution is uniquely Christian—so Canadian Christians in the 21st century have yet to unite behind a comprehensive vision that is compelling enough to overturn the growing influence of Secularism's demand for the subjugation of all people to their worldview. This is very disturbing because the vision of Secularism is a deceptive, totalitarian vision advanced behind the rhetoric of a hyper-pluralism—rhetoric that gives the impression that its proponents are moving away from tyranny, towards cooperation, tolerance and moderation. Nothing could be further from the truth.

Christians should be arguing for the centrality of Christian ethics in the formulation of the public policy and law of our nation. We need to re-educate ourselves about the morally superior nature of Christianity for law and public policy as well as for private morality, identifying the ways in which Christianity applies the grace of God in society.

Maybe we have something to learn from Christian members of Parliament in Australia. In a recent development, a 300-strong Christian forum was held at Parliament House in Australia with more than a dozen politicians attending. Former National Party leader John Anderson delivered a statement from current Australian Prime Minister John Howard, in which he "praised the contribution of Christianity and endorsed the

---

17. "We Have a Huge Stake in Christianity," by Paul Craig Roberts. *Human Events*, December 21, 2005. http://www.humaneventsonline.com/article.php?id=11029.

forum," according to a report in *The Australian*.[18] Although Mr. Anderson expressed support for the idea of a secular state, he did say that a free and democratic Australia was enjoying the fruits of a Christian value system, warning that "no fruit will survive without you tending the roots that provided the growth in the first place and without replanting." At the same event, Liberal Tasmanian Senator Guy Barnett said the conference had been stimulated in part by "the denigration at a public level of Christian values."

Christianity is the truth; it is God's redemptive message to mankind. If Christianity is a message of grace and mercy in terms of eternal and spiritual concerns, then it is also the source of grace and mercy for life in this world. How could a Christian argue otherwise? Applying Christian principles to public life, then, is a gracious and merciful thing to do, even if non-Christians do not recognize this to be true.[19]

Consider what Alexis de Tocqueville said about America. He traveled throughout the United States in the 1830s and published his findings in his renowned "Democracy in America," which "remains today the classic account of the moral aspirations, and dangers, of liberal democracy,"[20] noted Professor John von Heyking associate professor of political science, University of Lethbridge, at a June 2006 conference on the Cooperation of Church & State.

"He wrote that religion has a paradoxical relationship with the liberal state. On the one hand, the great achievement of

18. "Christian MPs meeting hits back at secularism," by Patricia Karvelas. *The Australian*, August 9, 2006.
19. This proposition is central to Chapter Four of this book and, hence, is developed in much more detail there.
20. "Politics Between the Earthly City and the City of God in Christianity," Paper presented by John von Heyking. The Centre for Cultural Renewal's Cooperation of Church & State Conference, Calgary, Alberta. June 8-9, 2006.

liberal democracy was its legal separation of political from religious power. On the other hand, the legal separation of church and state requires a social and cultural cooperation between the two."[21]

Unfortunately, the extremists of modern secularism believe that philosophical consistency requires one to advocate the social and cultural separation of church and state along with a legal separation. Or, perhaps secularists are just using the concept of the legal separation of church and state also to demand the social and cultural suppression of Christianity because they despise the faith. Whatever their ultimate motive and intention, the outcome is the same: intolerant absolutism and irrational persecution of those whose worldview is responsible for the democratic tradition.

Tocqueville correctly noted that "legal separation allows religion greater freedom to find its own authentic prophetic voice, which therefore enables citizens to restrain the moral claims of the state, thereby ensuring limited and free government,"[22] in the words of von Heyking.

"Tocqueville also argued that of all types of regime—including monarchy, aristocracy, and democracy—it is democracy that requires the greatest amount of moral virtue from its citizens. Morally speaking, it is easy to be a subject of a monarchy because one simply needs to obey the monarch's demands. Being a citizen of democracy demands self-government, and thus moral judgment, which is considerably more difficult to practise. Being a subject of a monarch simply requires moderation. Being a democratic citizen demands practical wisdom, courage, justice, as well as moderation."[23]

21. Ibid.
22. Ibid.
23. Ibid.

Tocqueville was entirely correct. Is it any wonder that militant secularism/atheism is bringing with it a spike in the level of intolerance, censorship and suppression of dissent? The morality of secularism is completely incompatible with "democracy."

Secularism's systemic hypocrisy

Another tactic of the Secular Humanist is vital to note: when Secularists want to decriminalize something, they label the current law as inherently religious, that is, Christian. The most obvious examples today are abortion and homosexuality. Secularists have framed the disputes over the criminal sanctions against these actions as a conflict between fundamentalist Christians and the rest of the world.

Secularists also strongly oppose the teaching of creation science in the classroom and they oppose the teaching of abstinence or chastity, which is simply one application of the virtue of self-restraint or self-government—a foundational characteristic of civilized men and a healthy society. Secularists also champion other deviant practices such as drug abuse, gambling, prostitution and, increasingly, pedophilia.[24] Meanwhile, they marginalize opposition to their public policy agenda by claiming that it is rooted in fundamentalist, old-fashioned, strident, narrow-minded, conservative Christianity. They claim that the legislation they are fighting is inherently religious.

[24] Resolutions were debated in the last Liberal Party of Canada policy conference to decriminalize prostitution and some crimes pertaining to drug use. New Democrat MP Libby Davies has been championing the cause of legalizing prostitution for several years. The UN revoked the Non-Governmental Organization (NGO) status of ILGA (International Lesbian and Gay Association) because of their affiliation with the pedophile group NAMBLA (North American Man/Boy Love Association). ILGA, however, continues to lobby to regain its NGO status as though this is not sufficient cause to ostracize the organization. And in Canada, Secularists keep advancing the most specious arguments against the Conservative government's attempts to raise the age of sexual consent from 14 to 16 in order to protect young teens from sexual predators.

This tactic is designed to identify the value as singularly Christian in nature, and therefore, allegedly incompatible with a pluralistic society, a society that supposedly has to govern on the basis of values that are broadly accepted by the populace. Secular Humanists transpose *their* rejection of a particular moral standard onto the general public, arguing that it is the non-Christian general public, not simply themselves, who have a problem with such a law, so it needs to be abandoned. Marginalizing the law as inherently Christian helps to expedite this process of overturning it while simultaneously doing away with the need to provide a rational defence for the Secularist position. After all, people do not need an argument if they can be stirred up to agree with you at an emotional level.

Interestingly, however, you will not see many Secular Humanists condemning laws against rape, murder, theft, assault and vandalism. Yet historically, the laws that we have against these offences originated in the same Christian worldview that calls for the banning of abortion, homosexuality and prostitution and the strict regulating of divorce. It is true that other worldviews also ban rape, murder, theft and other vices deemed crimes by Christianity. Sometimes those principles fit logically with those other religions' foundational principles; sometimes, as in the case of Secularism, they are twisted, manipulated and coerced to fit in order to shore up an incoherent and inherently weak ideology. Whatever the case, historically these moral standards come to us in Canada via Christianity, so it is fundamentally dishonest of Secular Humanists to condemn Christianity's influence on certain aspects of public policy—and even on public policy in general—while strongly defending Canada's Christian laws against rape, murder, theft and the like. Hypocrisy is not

71

exclusive to Secular Humanism but it certainly holds a place of primacy in the Secularist moral order.

If Secular Humanists hate Christianity, let them have the integrity to condemn the whole package and expose themselves for the anti-rational zealots that they are. Instead, they try to shore up their image and preserve a perception of civility and intellectual coherence by co-opting many Christian virtues and benefits, pretending that such things are also compatible with Secular Humanism, rather than being religious in nature.

It is also fundamentally dishonest to marginalize Christianity as the embodiment of evil when Christianity is also what brought to Canada and the West the spirit of—and character development necessary for—entrepreneurship, industry and thrift as well as the charitable spirit that led to the founding of hospitals, orphanages and other charitable endeavours, not to mention the desire to educate people with the founding of schools and universities. Even today, the significantly Christian and post-Christian countries did more to help the Muslim victims of the tsunamis than the oil-rich Islamic countries did, as was noted by Christian apologist Chuck Colson.[25] And following the tragedy in New Orleans caused by Hurricane Katrina, Mr. Colson noted the same pattern:

---

25. "I also find it noteworthy that of the top ten countries, none is a Muslim nation. Just yesterday, Saudi Arabia agreed, after much public criticism, to triple its originally pledged $10 million…. By contrast, America with its Christian heritage is giving generously to non-Christian nations…. What happened in southeast Asia is… an apologetic opportunity: Let the world see the kind of compassion we have for all people, not just fellow Christians. At the same time, the world can plainly see the limitations of a religion like Islam—theocratic, closed, indifferent, and unconcerned about the needs of others, even in its own Muslim family. "A Heritage of Giving," by Charles Colson. Breakpoint, January 5, 2005.

People who have lost everything are staying in shelters. And who are running those shelters? Churches. Christians were the first to arrive on the scene—literally the first responders—the first to help with the devastation in New Orleans, even before the first government assistance arrived. And Christians shouldn't be surprised at this, even if reporters are. Because throughout history, Christians have been passionate about human dignity. We believe all humans are made in the image of God. This is why Christians throughout history have rescued abandoned babies, fought slavery, and passed child labor laws. Today, we care equally for the mother dying of AIDS in Africa, the six-year-old sex slave in Thailand, and the homeless family in New Orleans.[26]

On the other hand, today's Secular Humanists are so self-absorbed and greedy that their personal charitable donations remain paltry, so they try to salve their guilty consciences by demanding that governments make up the difference by coercively extracting tax dollars from their neighbours to make up for the charitable shortfall that results from their own selfishness. Even in our day, Secular Humanists have yet to develop a coherent model for effective education. The eroding academic standards and growing problems of violence and disrespect in today's Secular Humanist-controlled schools are a damning indictment of the ideology, as is the growing demand for home education and tutoring. If public schools were permitted to compete on an equal playing field with other alternatives, rather than being artificially propped

26. "Why Christians Are the 'First Responders'," by Charles Colson. Breakpoint, September 14, 2005.

up with expropriated taxpayer dollars, they would have collapsed years ago.

ABC News correspondent John Stossel has provided a very concise summary of the comprehensive degree of private charity that existed in the United States in the early 1900's before Secular Humanists began to remake America in their state-ist image. He wrote:

> I once thought there was too much poverty for private charity to make much of a difference. Now I realize that private charity would do much more—if government hadn't crowded it out. In the 1920s—the last decade before the Roosevelt administration launched its campaign to federalize nearly everything—30% of American men belonged to mutual aid societies, groups of people with similar backgrounds who banded together to help members in trouble. They were especially common among minorities. Mutual aid societies paid for doctors, built orphanages and cooked for the poor. Neighbors knew best what neighbors needed. They were better at making judgments about who needs a handout and who needed a kick in the rear. They helped the helpless, but administered tough love to the rest. They taught self-sufficiency.

> Mutual aid didn't solve every problem, so government stepped in. But government didn't solve every problem either. Instead, it caused more problems by driving private charity out. Today, there are fewer mutual-aid societies, because people say, "We already pay taxes for HUD, HHS. Let the professionals do

it." Big Government tells both the poor and those who would help them, "Don't try"... When you rely on the government to help those who need it, you don't practise benevolence yourself. You don't take responsibility for deciding whom to help. Just as public assistance discourages the poor from becoming independent by rewarding them with fixed handouts, it discourages the rest of us from being benevolent. This may be the greatest irony of the welfare state: It not only encourages the poor to stay dependent, it kills individuals' desire to help them.

The point with these various examples of irrationality in Secular Humanist thought is to show that Secular Humanists, intentionally or otherwise, use rhetorical sleight of hand to advance their agenda. Their deception and ignorance is specifically targeted at Christianity because it is the Christian foundations of this country that they are trying to overturn and replace. Christians need to understand the nature of Secular Humanism, including the nature of its arguments so that they can effectively combat this dangerous ideology. Secular Humanism is unsustainable, but the more influence it gains in society before collapsing, the more harm it will cause to people as it self-destructs. Christians who take their responsibility to be the incarnation of God's grace in society are obligated to combat this cancerous agenda rather than cooperating with it and allowing it to run its course. We do this by infusing our politics with our religion; by being faithful to Christian principles in our public lives as well as our private lives, including the way we actively participate in the governance, law-making and public policy process in Canada. Christians who abandon this sphere to others are denying a fundamental aspect of their faith in God.

Ted Byfield addressed this issue in a very good column in January 2005.[27] His comments deserve extended citation here. He was responding to the comments of Cabinet Minister Pierre Pettigrew as noted at the outset of this chapter:

> ... Pettigrew says, the two cardinals are intervening in the affairs of the government, and should, in effect, "butt out." In short, no one should be allowed to cite religious authority in the formation of government policy. What the Bible says or the Koran or churches, or the synagogues, must not be allowed to influence the content of Canadian law.

> That's not only the minister's position, but also that of the liberal media. However, none of them seem to have taken this dictum to its inevitable conclusion. All laws—not just laws concerning sexual behavior—are based upon some moral principle. The entire Criminal Code, for starters, is an anthology of morality. Thou shalt not steal, thou shalt not lie, thou shalt not murder, all these rules are moral principles. But their scope is much broader than that. The tax laws all stand on the moral principle that everybody has a responsibility to pay for the services of the government. The income tax law stands on the further moral principle that how much we pay should be determined by how much we make. All the laws on corporate finance are there to prevent fraud, theft and extortion. They rest, that is,

27. "Pettigrew puts boots to religious Canadians," by Ted Byfield. *The Calgary Sun*, January 30, 2005.

on the moral assumption that these things are wrong. The bylaws that require you to weed your garden and shovel your snow rest on the moral principle that you should protect your neighbour and his property.

The first point to note then is this: morality does not lie behind some of the things legislators do. It lies behind everything they do, because every law is an attempt to enforce—coercively—some moral principle. The second point is equally important. The basis of the morality of just about everybody in the country is religious. We don't steal and we don't murder because the Bible says we shouldn't. When we send money to relieve the victims of the tsunami, it's because we're trying to love our neighbour, a biblical injunction. If we seek to make education available to everyone, it's because we think it's "fair," and what we think "fair," whether we realize it or not, comes directly out of the Bible.

Therefore, when Pettigrew says that religion must not be allowed to influence public policy, he disqualifies from participation in government all those whose moral basis lies in religion. Since our religion is ultimately the only reason we can give for favouring, or opposing, any law, he has in reality called for the disenfranchisement of just about every Canadian. And nobody in cabinet bats an eyelash. Welcome to the New Canada.

The bottom line is that Christianity is superior to other faiths and worldviews. Its contributions to culture, political theory and public morality gave us civilization and societies that are the envy of genuinely oppressed people everywhere.[28]

28. Another area which demonstrates the superiority of Christianity is the general moral debasement of culture by way of the "sexualization" of public life by homosexual activists and Secular Humanists. We saw numerous examples of this with federal politicians in 2006. In July, *Maclean's* magazine reported on a "Liberal Leadership Wet T-Shirt Contest" ("Capital Diary," By Mitchel Raphael. July 24, 2006). "At this year's gay Pride celebrations in Toronto, Nova Scotia MP Scott Brison… sold Liberal memberships at the event in support of his leadership bid. He appeared to be the only leadership candidate with his own booth. Among his male volunteers, those who had the sleeves cut off their T-shirts sold more party memberships than those who did not. … The Liberals held aloft a giant Canadian flag and dodged red water balloons that were lobbed at them from rooftops. Michael Ignatieff, a popular target, got soaked. Martha Hall Findlay brought her own water gun. "The only warning I got was, 'Don't wear a white T-shirt at Pride,' said Hall Findlay. … Was she afraid the Liberal leadership race would degenerate into a wet T-shirt contest? … Belinda Stronach marched with the gay rights lobby Egale Canada and blew bubbles with Rick Mercer, also with the group …" The Liberal leadership contest also saw full body rear video footage of leadership candidate Bob Rae running naked into the water with comedian Rick Mercer and Scott Brison appearing nude in a fundraising calendar. On *Maclean's* supplemental news service on their website, columnist Mitchel Raphael posted a picture of Olivia Chow, MP for the Toronto riding of Trinity-Spadina, and wife of New Democrat Party leader Jack Layton, sitting between two semi-dressed models whose legs are draped over hers ("One MP on fetish party/fashion show VIP list." *Capital Diary: Outtakes.* October 26, 2006. http://forums.macleans.ca/advansis/?mod=for&act=dis&eid=30&so=1&sb=1&ps=60). This is what constitutes humour and entertainment in today's neo-barbarian age of over-stimulated adult adolescents. And these are politicians, "poster boys" of the Secularist vision!

CHAPTER THREE

CLEARING UP TWO OTHER MYTHS
ABOUT THE SEPARATION OF CHURCH AND STATE

Church leaders must speak to the civil government

A second area in which the separation of church and state is incorrectly applied is in attempts to inhibit church leaders—clergy—from speaking publicly on matters being considered by the civil government. This is reflected in some of the comments critical of clergy input into issues being considered by Parliament—at least when the clergy comments reflect a conservative critique. The homosexual "marriage" controversy has given rise to many criticisms of clergy comments as well as of church sanctions levelled by clergy against some homosexual "marriage"-supporting politicians.

This opposition to clergy participation in public debate has also been identified as the rationale behind inquiries made by the Canada Customs and Revenue Agency (Canada's tax officials) into the comments of church officials on so-called political issues during the 2004 election. The CCRA, for example, contacted Calgary Roman Catholic Bishop Fred Henry over a pastoral letter that he wrote and posted on his diocesan website saying that Prime Minister Paul Martin was not a good Catholic. CCRA officials also met with the Evangelical Fellowship of Canada. They were supposedly concerned about partisanship, a no-no for charitable organizations when they venture into comment on "political" issues. The CCRA denies allegations of nefarious motives. The relevance of such investigations is that the government could revoke the charitable tax status of churches and parachurch organizations that violate charitable tax law by making supposedly partisan comments on political issues.

Roman Catholic Calgary Bishop Fred Henry, the lightning rod today for Secular Humanists' hostility towards Christianity, responded succinctly to this kind of criticism in an interview with *Western Standard* magazine[1]. He said: "I'm simply saying, look, we don't ask the psychologist to leave aside his Freudian psychology when he enters into the political realm. We don't ask, say, a labour union rep to lay aside his principles in terms of espousing labour unions. … [The separation argument] is an attempt to try and marginalize people and say: 'You're religious, you have nothing really to contribute,' we should remain silent. Well, I think we have a lot to contribute."

The Confessions in the Reformed Christian tradition address the rightful role and function of the civil magistrate. The Scottish Presbyterian tradition holds to the *Westminster Confession of Faith*, and the specific denominational tradition

---

1. "Question Period." *Western Standard*, May 2, 2005

of this author also subscribes to the *Testimony of the Reformed Presbyterian Church of North America*. This Confession makes several declarations regarding the rightful authority of church leaders to speak to the political experience of their day. For example, it declares: "Both the Christian and the Church have a responsibility for witnessing against national sins and for promoting justice. Amos 2:6-8; 5:14-15" (Chapter 23, #22). Elsewhere it declares: "It is the duty of the Christian Church to testify to the authority of Christ over the nations, against all anti-Christian, atheistic, and Secular principles of civil government, and against sinful oaths of allegiance to civil governments. When the Church by orderly processes in her own courts determines that the oath of allegiance to a civil government compromises the Christian's loyalty to Christ or involves the Christian in the support of sinful principles of civil government, the Church must require her members to refuse such sinful oaths. Acts 4:24-29; Ephesians 5:11; Revelation 3:15-16; Acts 15:28-29; Revelation 2:13-14" (Chapter 23, #28).

Some Christian traditions simply assert their view as, "No creed but Christ." But even here, one looks to a biblical passage such as the account where Jesus says, "Give to Caesar what is Caesar's and to God what is God's." In this statement, Christ is asserting emphatically that there are areas of life over which the state has no legitimate claim of authority. Faithful Christian elders must—and will—assert and re-assert their rightful authority over the governmental responsibilities of the Church. They will not willingly surrender this authority to totalitarian Secular Humanism, which claims the right of the state to impose its control over any and every entity that influences the work of civil magistrates.

We have to remember that politicians are still men; they are not gods. Civil magistrates are mere men who must come before God to be judged in the same manner as all men. The church has the same role towards them as it does towards all other men, calling them to repent of their sin and to turn to God, submitting their lives to Him for redemption, and committing themselves to live under His law for the remainder of their lives.

Clergy oversee the mission of their congregations, and are responsible to ensure that they remain faithful to the mission God has given the Church. In so doing, they are responsible for ensuring that church members uphold their vows as faithful members of the Christian community. If church members abandon this commitment, the church has a discipline process and various sanctions to use to bring wayward members back in line—or to impose judgment on them if they refuse to repent. Hence, when governors who have become members of the church violate the terms of their membership vows and their profession of faith, they must be dealt with in the same fashion as any other church member by the church leadership.[2]

The final expression of that discipline is excommunication, in which case your membership is revoked and, according to Christian doctrine, you are bearing evidence that you are estranged from God and at risk of eternal damnation. This is the nature of the threat that hangs over politicians when the Roman Catholic church threatens to withhold Communion from Catholic politicians who support homosexual "marriage." When clergy issue this threat, they are acting within the parameters of church government as ordained by God (and

2. This is an application of the principle of equality before the law, an ethic that Secularists abhor although, by radically redefining the term, they have stolen it to use in manipulating people to support their equality-hating worldview. It is Secular Humanists who promote patronage, (reverse) racism and other forms of favouritism and preferential treatment.

still permitted in Canada). Hence, it is the height of arrogance and evidence of the most extreme vision of socialistic centralism when politicians and other Secular Humanists condemn clergy for issuing those warnings, objecting that such threats can illegitimately influence public policy.

Of course counsel from religious leaders can influence public policy. An automobile accident can keep a Member of Parliament from getting to the House of Commons in time for an important vote. What are Secular Humanists going to do next? Ban traffic accidents?

This criticism from Secularists is actually amusing when one considers the childish level of irrationality that it exposes. When Catholic leaders call Catholic politicians to respect their faith commitment in their public policy work, they are not putting a gun to these politicians' heads and telling them that they have to remain Catholic. The premise is, "If you are going to keep self-identifying as a Catholic, then …" If these politicians do not want to be faithful to Catholic doctrine in their public policy work, then they can always turn in their Catholic membership certificate and stop calling themselves Catholic.

I do not hear Secularists telling Catholic politicians to just abandon their professed Catholic allegiance. "To tell a Catholic politician to reject his Catholic faith and Catholic roots would be a violation of religious freedom," is probably the answer one would get to such a suggestion.

So, it is a violation of religious freedom to tell a Catholic politician to abandon his Catholic profession, but it is not a violation of religious freedom to tell a Catholic politician that he is not allowed to bring his faith commitment to bear on his public policy work. See how long it takes to go loony trying to get your mind around that example of Secularist anti-rationality.

The influence of ecclesiastical decisions on politicians and public policy is not supposed to be the concern of clergy one way or the other in the exercise of their governmental leadership over the Church of Jesus Christ. The Church's primary concern is a person's eternal salvation. And they also have an obligation to speak authoritatively on moral questions. When religious leaders speak to issues and challenge politicians, their general moral direction may well carry obvious implications for certain votes on legislation, but religious leaders rarely, if ever, tell politicians specifically how to vote. It is, therefore, grossly dishonest, and in some cases probably fraudulent, the way some critics charge that the Pope and other religious leaders are actually dictating to politicians how to vote.

As noted, moral teaching that speaks to current issues may have obvious implications for voting, but that is because life is not atomized; it is integrated. That is a fundamental component of reality. As noted repeatedly in this publication, Secularism has an abiding aversion to rationality—but it is about time it decided to take reality seriously. Yes, religion impacts politics—whether the religion of Christianity, or the religion of Secularism, or Judaism, or Hinduism or any other religion. That is an unchangeable fact of life, not a matter of decree or human decision. Secularists who want to stamp out the impact of Christian religion on politics (under the dishonest rhetoric of separation of Church and State) are, in fact, arguing for a ban on Christian politicians. Do the majority of Canadians support such a bigoted and transparently offensive proposition? No! That is why most Secularists do not come out and say what they really mean. Instead they dress up their hate in all kinds of irrational euphemisms.

People who challenge the legitimacy of clergy decisions motivated by concern over redemption, because of their potential ancillary impact on public policy, are saying that political considerations should be given primacy over spiritual considerations. In other words, they are saying that the perspective of Secular Humanism should be treated as normative, subordinating the Christian view of reality to their dictates—even in terms of how clergy think and behave.

This Secularist status quo has become entrenched to a disturbing degree in Canada's collective conscience. In the fall of 2005, Catholic columnist Michael Coren wrote an article on the obligation of Catholic politicians—e.g. former Liberal Prime Minister Paul Martin—to honour their church's doctrines. The article, published in the *London Free Press*, generated at least two letters of condemnation from London-area residents. Obviously, believing themselves to be decent and literate advocates of democracy and fairness, these letter writers, in fact, advocated for tyrannical Secularism; that is, state-ist centralism.

One of the letter writers wrote:

> ... Michael Coren states that Prime Minister Paul Martin should not receive communion if he does not back the position of the Catholic Church on moral issues—specifically, gay marriage. Once again, Coren has decided to disregard the fact that the Canadian political system and the Catholic Church are not, in fact, one in (sic) the same. Martin works for the people

of Canada. He is not a church employee. Religion is not a universal entity. Each purports its own teachings, its own beliefs. The Canadian political system must, by its very nature, strive to be a universal entity for Canadians. There is no way a governing system of law can be effective if it does not strive to work in the best interests of all people under its rule. That includes people of all religions, cultures, economic classes, sex and, yes, sexualities.

Martin has simply recognized that he cannot allow the doctrines of his religion, or those of any other politician, to interfere with the rights of the population as a whole. Religion is a personal matter. Much like an individual's opinion, it does not need to be fair, impartial or inclusive. Politics, however, is a public matter. The political system has an obligation to all of those it serves to promote fairness, impartiality and inclusiveness. Pope Benedict did, indeed, say it beautifully. "A tolerance which allows God as a private opinion but which excludes Him from public life, from the reality of the world and our lives, is not tolerance but hypocrisy." The same, Mr. Coren, can be said of homosexuality and gay marriage.[3]

This writer sees every relationship that a person has as necessarily subservient to his relationship to the state. This is especially true for politicians. This person is so intellectually blind that he treats his position as absolutely true—you can feel the dogmatism throughout his letter—yet relativists are not supposed to believe in absolute truth! This London, Ontario, resident is a disciple of atheistic Secularism. This ideology of state-ist centralism is tyrannical, not democratic.

3. "Good reason to keep church, state separate." *The London Free Press*, October 13, 2006.

The other letter writer was just as dogmatic—and just as confused:

> An electorate does not choose a politician to do what his church dictates. He/she is elected to represent the constituents and carry out their wishes. Even if a church's teaching is directly opposite his voters' wishes, he has no choice but to abide by the directions of those who elected him. Coren says Prime Minister Paul Martin "disobeyed his church." But Martin obeyed his constituents. Coren says Martin did not allow his cabinet "to vote according to their conscience," but argues that Martin should not be allowed to vote his conscience. If you follow Coren's "logic," then no person subject to any dictatorial religion should run for public office, because sooner or later there could be a conflict. Penalizing a politician for following the directions of his/her constituents belittles the religion in question. Since when were the clergy elected to run our country?[4]

see p 90

see p. 90

The arrogance of this tyrannical position is astounding. Where is Secularism's spirit of compromise? Where is Secularism's "neutral meeting ground" for the development of pluralistic public values? It does not exist. And it does not exist in orthodox Christianity either. Christians need to abandon their defeatist posture and their commitment to the illegitimate kind of compromise demanded by Secular Humanism in the real world of law and public policy development.

As outrageous as such comments are, in some respects these kinds of criticisms are as amusing as they are ignorant. The above writer may be a supporter of populism, but many of

see p. 90

4. "Church not elected to run the country." *The London Free Press*, October 13, 2006.

those people who oppose social conservative public policy are the same people who condemned the old Reform Party's populist proposals. At the time, many Liberal Members of Parliament, for example, would condemn proposals for such provisions as referenda and MP recall, arguing that politicians should show leadership by articulating positions on various issues and sticking with them instead of going to the people every single time they have a hard issue to address. Yet many of those same people today, inventing a false dichotomy, are arguing that politicians are elected to represent their constituents, not their church.

The fact is that many things influence a person's beliefs, including his religious allegiance. Normally, the totality of these beliefs is what attracts a would-be politician to a particular political party in the first place and, then, to articulate the various views he presents while running for office against the candidates from other parties. Sometimes people are interested in the underlying influences of a politician's beliefs, but for the most part, such questions do not come up on the hustings these days. How many people care whether a politician's support for throwing child sexual abusers in jail comes from a profound Christian conviction, a loose Christian conviction, Secularist beliefs or an Islamic framework? If a Catholic politician votes for real marriage because that is his conviction based, to whatever degree, on Catholic principles, then it does not make his vote any less legitimate because such a vote comes three days after the Pope or a bishop speaks out on the issue. And if his constituents did not know that he would vote for marriage, but that is an important issue for them, then that is their problem, not his. This supposed dichotomy between allegiance to the Church and allegiance to constituents is just another rhetorical weapon in the arsenal of bigoted Secularists.

It is also important to note that, while Secular Humanists condemn the Church for acting within its lawful parameters, because by doing so, it is influencing politicians in their political work—and, therefore, is allegedly overstepping its legitimate jurisdiction—Secularist politicians have no problem legislating in such a fashion as to encroach on the Church's jurisdiction, restricting the religious liberty of the clergy. We have seen this clearly with the advancement of the homosexual "marriage" agenda[5]. The hypocrisy is astounding, but the reason for it is that Secularists deify the state, so the civil magistrate becomes the central organizing entity for human society and everything man does must be subsumed to the demands and jurisdiction of the civil government.

The intersection of church and state

One of the most articulate explanations of the Christian teaching about the intersection of the church and the state that I have heard recently is that articulated by Tristan Emmanuel, the founder and president of the ECP Centre (Equipping Christians for the Public-square Centre). In a message based on the biblical passage, First Timothy, chapter 2, verses 1-4, he talks about the duty of the civil magistrate to provide a social environment of peace primarily for the purpose of advancing the Kingdom of God, and the duty of Christians to call the civil government to that function.

---

5. This is evident not only in the behaviour of Canada's tax officials towards Bishop Fred Henry and the EFC, but also in the betrayal of traitorous clergy such as British Columbia's Anglican bishop Michal Ingham, who objects to religious liberty provisions: "It means that if you're a non-believer, you cannot discriminate against gay and lesbians, but if you're a believer you can. So if you want to discriminate against gays and lesbian people, join a religious organization." ("Religious same-sex discrimination worries bishop," CBC, December 9, 2004.)

I Timothy 2:1-4 (King James Version) reads as follows:

> I exhort therefore, that, first of all, supplications, prayers, intercessions, and giving of thanks, be made for all men; For kings, and for all that are in authority; that we may lead a quiet and peaceable life in all godliness and honesty. For this is good and acceptable in the sight of God our Saviour; Who will have all men to be saved, and to come unto the knowledge of the truth.

Explaining the passage, Mr. Emmanuel says that Paul's instruction to Timothy is: "'In the setting of a worship service'—a public assembly—'the first thing I want you to do is to pray for your countrymen, especially kings—all those in authority.' How often have I been in a worship service where this is done? And we wonder why we have the government we have."

Mr. Emmanuel goes on to discuss the purpose Paul gives for praying for those in authority over us:

> "You need to pray, Timothy, for the kings and those in authority because ..." Remember the context! First century Rome: A very hostile environment for these Christians. Persecution was now coming for real. Rome had a Caesar who was going after the apostle Paul and all Christians. At this point, they were beginning to realize what was on the horizon for them; that it was not going to be easy. And Paul says: "I want you to pray for the kings, for those in authority." Why? So that they can be blessed as kings, so that they can arrogate to themselves more wealth, pomp and circumstance? No. "Pray, so that you can live at peace in your society. But not just so you can live a comfortable life where

nobody is going to bother you." That's not the point. It is much more than that. "Pray for those in authority that we may live a quiet and peaceable life in all godliness and reverence" … Now notice: This is the ultimate aim of praying for those in authority: "… for this is good and acceptable in the sight of God our Saviour Who desires all men to be saved, to come to the knowledge of the truth."

Mr. Emmanuel then begins to apply the message, demonstrating the importance of Christian participation in the public square and Christian leadership in the culture. He points out that, with Bill C-250, the federal government has directly interfered with one of the core responsibilities of the Church, preaching the Gospel. This alone demonstrates the absurdity of any claim that religion and politics are, or can be, separate and distinct realms of life:

> Here is where Paul answers the question of whether there really is a separation between politics and faith, and his answer is unequivocal: "No!"

> I have never read a more political prayer in my life. Think about it. He's saying, "I want you to beseech the sovereign Lord of the universe—the King of Kings. I want you to ask the King of Kings to wrest the heart of the Roman Caesar—to change his heart—so that you as Christians will be free from persecution, so that you can concentrate on what you need to be doing, and that is to get out there and share the Gospel."

> … As Paul points out, the government has been vested with the power to create a society that is stable and at peace—where liberty reigns—or it has

the power to suppress and create chaos. That's the kind of power the state has. God gave the state that power. In Genesis, chapter 9, we are told the state is vested with the sword to establish peace between men because God knows that men naturally are prone to want to hurt each other, prone to want to enslave each other: they're prone to want to do all kinds of wicked things. So God created the state for the very purpose of creating an orderly society in the temporal realm. But, of course, the state can be used to advance evil. And that's why it is so important to pray of the Lord: "Lord, please, I beg of You, have mercy on the people. Change our government. Make our government sound. Make our government committed to morality. Make our government committed to protecting inalienable liberties." One of these inalienable liberties is our right to share the Gospel and to protect created ordinances like marriage.

Explaining the relevance of this priority for Canadians, Mr. Emmanuel said (speaking while the previous Liberal government was in power):

Right now, in Canada, we have a government that is not interested in protecting these liberties. We have, in fact, a government that passed a law that, on paper, makes it a crime now to criticize homosexual orientation, or the behaviour thereof—to level a moral or biological criticism against this sexual preference. Did you know that? That bill was called Bill C-250. The government believes that there is a minority group in Canada that is constantly subject to hate crime and vilification under the guise of religion, so they passed this bill that will basically make it criminal to criticize these homosexuals.

What I submit to you is that here we have an example, in law, of a government that is actually suppressing a liberty that we have been given by God. What is that liberty? To preach the Gospel. You cannot preach the Gospel to homosexuals, or to anyone enslaved in any sexual sin, if you do not have the liberty to tell them the bad news first. People, in our culture, do not understand why they need Jesus, and the reason they do not understand is that they do not see the moral problem they have. They do not believe they are morally bankrupt. They do not believe they are morally bankrupt because, frankly, the laws of this nation are systematically rewriting morality. It all begins with the law. The law is a teacher in that respect.

In concluding his teaching on I Timothy 2:1-4, Mr. Emmanuel explained that in the context of Roman rule into which Paul was speaking, prayer was all that Christians could do at the time. While it is still the most important duty of Christians, he argues that what it reflects is an attitude that does not simply accept persecution as an inevitable reality. So he says that Christians today, taking hold of that biblical attitude, are obligated under God to do a lot more, engaging in all lawful political activity that is available to us.

In Paul's day, … they were not free citizens. They did not have the right to vote. They did not have the freedom to pick the Caesar they wanted. They had no democratic rights. Paul knew they did not need to have democratic rights to see things change in Rome. They prayed to the King of Kings. But you and I, 2,000 years later, have inherited a great freedom. What have we to show for it?

The apostle's words are a stinging indictment against us because of our lack of genuine concern for our country and for future generations that will be born under a policy that endorses perversion. We can not only pray for the next generation of Canadians, we have the freedom, and the responsibility, now before it is too late, to stand up and defend marriage.

CHAPTER FOUR

WHAT IS MEANT BY THE SEPARATION OF CHURCH AND STATE

B oth the government of the nation and the government of the visible church are established by God. Though distinct and independent of each other, they both owe supreme allegiance to Jesus Christ. The governments of church and state differ in sphere of authority in that due submission to the government of the visible church is the obligation of members thereof, while due submission to civil government is the obligation of all men. The governments of church and state also have different functions and prerogatives in the advancement of the Kingdom of God. The means of enforcement of the civil government are physical, while those of church government are not. Neither government has the right to invade or assume the authority of the other. They should cooperate to the honor and glory of God, while maintaining their separate jurisdictions. Rom.

13:1; Matt. 22:21; Col. 1:18; Acts 15:10; Ezra 7:10, 25-26; 2 Chron. 26: 18-19; Matt. 5:25; 1 Cor. 5:12-13. (*The Testimony of the Reformed Presbyterian Church of North America*, Chapter 23, #19)

... [The civil rulers] should do this while completely refraining from every tendency toward exercising absolute authority, and while functioning in the sphere entrusted to them, with the means belonging to them. (*The Belgic Confession of Faith*, Article 36)

The above is an excellent summary of what is meant by the Christian doctrine of the separation of church and state. It flows out of a broader concept that also recognizes the existence and function of the other divine covenantal institution, the family. Along with self-government, God has given us three social governmental institutions that have their own spheres of authority, often understood within the framework identified as "sphere sovereignty." We have family government, church government and civil government. The spheres of authority of these institutions intersect, but where they do, they exercise different types of authority. For example, if someone is found guilty of murder, the state has the authority to impose criminal penalties, including capital punishment. Church governments and family governments have no biblical authority to impose criminal sanctions. A church's final level of imposing sanctions is excommunication, revoking a person's membership in the church. This judgment is a declaration that the person is unrepentant regarding serious sin and is no longer recognized as a Christian by the church. Parents have sanctions they can impose to punish and hopefully restore sinful children. Ultimately, they can kick their child out of their home and terminate his access to the family inheritance. They also have recourse to corporal punishment, or spanking.

In today's socialist or Secular Humanist society, however, most people do not recognize a governmental role for the family. Consistent with such a development, the civil government over the past several decades has usurped most of this governmental responsibility from parents. We call it the social welfare state. It is the attempt by the civil government to be everybody's father and mother of last resort – although today it is no longer simply a last resort. With cradle-to-grave welfare, plans to expand taxpayer-funded daycare and state monopolization of the delivery of so-called medically necessary health care—not to mention the almost complete transference of control over sexual morality to the state—we have the almost complete usurpation by the state of parental responsibility for children. Hence, parent-imposed sanctions have almost all been gutted of their influence in the lives of children—an influence designed to bring them to conviction of sin and to lead them to repentance and restoration. As a result, we have a growing problem of family break-up with a growing number of single individuals who lack basic life skills, the training necessary to earn a liveable wage and the maturity to participate as respectful, responsible adults in society. In other words, the state's usurpation of family government is fuelling state dependency (by adult children) and a dangerous level of anarchy and social upheaval. It is all part of Secular Humanism's rejection of the principle of the separation of church and state.

These spheres of authority between the church, the state and the family can and do intersect in the lives of individuals because each person has a relationship of some sort with each of these institutions. Yet, the spheres of authority are distinct. The officers who exercise authority in these institutions are not supposed to be competing with each other for the control over any particular area of life. One can illustrate this point by looking at the structure of a business. It is very difficult for a business to be run effectively if people do not know what their own job descriptions are and do not know what the responsibilities of their colleagues are. If their responsibilities keep changing, that only makes matters worse. The same is the case in every area of society. When the civil government tries to exercise a role in the area of childcare, guaranteeing prices or wages, helping the homeless, or defining marriage, it is interfering in another jurisdiction, or sphere of authority. This causes conflict, and if it persists, it will lead to greater conflict, or the surrender by one authority to the other. As the socialist vision of Secular Humanism has advanced, the civil government has demanded ever more surrender by family government and church government of those areas that are rightfully directed by them. Regretfully, Christians have been far too quick to surrender to the advancing forces of their enemy.

This image of intersecting circles reflects the Biblical model of the relationship between civil government, church government and family government.

The Christian "sphere sovereignty" model of society can be pictured as intersecting circles with each form of government on an equal plane with the others, none exercising absolute authority over any other. The socialist picture for the structure of society is that of a pyramid, with the state, or civil government, perched at the top of the structure, governing every area of life, and subordinating everything else to itself. Socialism, therefore, is structured for tyranny—for oppression. It is antithetical to—completely incompatible with—Christianity and the liberty principle that flows from it.

This idea, then, of the distinct governmental roles of the church and the state, is the wonderful Christian doctrine of the separation of church and state. It is a concept that is fundamentally related to the other Christian teachings that provide civilizations with liberty and justice, principles such as equality before the law, freedom of conscience and freedom of religion; principles buttressed by mechanisms that flow out of principles such as division of authority, decentralization and localism.

In the next chapter we shall look in more detail at the need to roll back Secular Humanism and its agenda of tyranny by fighting to rein in the state to its legitimate sphere of authority, with the church and the family reclaiming the territory they have lost over the past few decades.

CHAPTER FIVE

THE STATE HAS NO BUSINESS IN THE BOARDROOMS OF THE NATION

The state has no business in the bedrooms of the nation, or the boardrooms of the nation, or the kitchens, or the kennels, or the backyards, or the living rooms of the nation.

Separation of church and state works both ways. It means that the church should not interfere in the affairs of the state, and that the state should not interfere in the affairs of the church. Those who scream, "Separation of church and state," however, are invariably only interested in one side of this coin—keeping the church out of what they claim to be the legitimate affairs of the state. They are, however, as we shall see, zealous to the extreme in their goal of interposing the state into the biblically-sanctioned governmental jurisdictions of the church and the family. This is evidence of the inherently socialistic nature of today's Secular Humanist political establishment—not to mention their blatant hypocrisy.

Their call for the separation of church and state is inconsistent and, therefore, intellectually dishonest. It is, in fact, simply a rhetorical veil behind which they are advancing their true agenda, the advancement of an all-pervasive state. Unfortunately, they are not meeting much resistance because today, even among Christians, a working knowledge of the governmental components of the nature of the church and the family is almost non-existent. Christians today also fail to make the robust biblical argument for the primacy of self-government, which under girds the governmental structure of society.

Christians, however, must rediscover this comprehensive cultural vision if they want to be able to offer Canadians a coherent, all-encompassing and practical vision of liberty in place of the dangerous agenda being imposed on them today by Secularists. Christians must rediscover this cultural vision simply to keep Canadian civilization alive because, without a broad-based commitment to self-government, a society cannot survive. It is fundamentally impossible to impose sufficient external constraints on people who do not already feel constrained to civil behaviour by internal compulsion. Not that anyone would want to live under such a fascistic and ruthless regime in the first place. Only Christians can lead Canada back—or forward—to such a civil order again, if they are prepared to do so.

Today's primary controversy, the battle to advance homosexual "marriage," is a perfect example of the Secularist agenda to impose the power and authority of the state beyond its legitimate sphere of authority. This agenda is a gross violation of the principle behind the idea of separation of church and state. The definition of marriage was given to us by God.

To redefine it is a pretension to deity and an expression of idolatry—the Secularist worship of the state as god. God gave the definition of marriage first to the family. Changing that definition of marriage throws the family into turmoil, and is a serious violation of the state's authority as it seeks to interpose itself on the lawful jurisdiction of family government. It is hard to imagine a more radical violation of the principle of sphere sovereignty—the principle that underlies the idea of the separation of church and state—than the push in Canada today to redefine marriage.

Does that mean that the state has no jurisdiction over marriage? Not at all (and this will be discussed later, in the next chapter), but the state has no legitimate authority, biblically speaking, to define marriage. Rather, it is expected to accept the definition God has supplied, and to affirm that definition in those areas where it has authority to address marriage. Marriage provides an example of the intersecting-circle model of society proposed by Christian theology. Each governmental body has a role in marriage—though distinct roles. We know from the Bible that divorce should be dealt with by the civil government, as should some types of extra-marital sexual relations, because some of the penalties related to divorce and these sexual offences involve criminal sanctions which church governments and family governments do not have the biblical authority to impose. By the implications of its role in the punishment of some offences against marriage, we understand that the state has a legitimate role in defending genuine marriage. The state does not have the authority to define marriage, but it does have a legitimate and necessary role in affirming and supporting the institution of marriage as defined by God, and revealed to us in the Bible. "Privatizing" marriage is not a legitimate biblical option.

Does the Bible teach deference to civil government or to self-government?

At this point, some people may argue that the Bible and Christian tradition are not very clear as to the legitimate parameters of authority between the family, the church and the state. That may be true in some cases, so it is worthwhile at this point to discuss what the broader theological framework should be for evaluating the parameters of jurisdictional authority in areas where the Bible seems to be unclear. Most of us lack the time to evaluate what to believe comprehensively at every point, so we develop philosophical or theological frameworks into which we can more quickly drop in various particulars, in order to arrive at conclusions with which we can feel fairly comfortable. This is legitimate "short-cut" thinking, at least temporarily.

In terms of our current discussion, most of us, I suspect, tend to give deference to the civil magistrate when determining where authority should lie in a particular area of life because we have been taught to think this way and we live in a context in which almost everyone else operates with that assumption. So, when in doubt, we tend not to defer to self-government, family government or church government, but rather to civil government. And when we appeal to the civil government to deal with a certain problem area, the tendency is to look to the national government rather than provincial and local governments. How many times have you heard criticisms, for example, of the "patchwork" of different regulations governing some area of health, education or the environment, with someone arguing for "national standards?" How many times have you bought into that argument without substantively analyzing the situation yourself?

If the media uncovers an apparent problem in society, particularly related to health, safety or the environment, it takes barely 24 hours for enough people to be mobilized to support legislation to deal with that issue. Meanwhile, those who instead advocate personal responsibility and self-government are treated as callous, uncaring extremists. Furthermore, instead of such disagreements leading to reasonable discussions about the best means to accomplish the ends of health, safety or a cleaner environment, the state-ist Secularists launch tirades of vicious rhetoric, accusing the advocates of personal liberty of being anti-environment and anti-health. Such is the degree of "intellectual rigor" one can expect from today's Secularists!

This presumption of state-ism is completely antithetical to the mentality that the Bible challenges us to have. We learn both from biblical teaching and from the trajectory of history that the Christian mentality should reflect a greater deference toward self-government, with a greater presumption towards family government and church government than towards civil government. Further, the emphasis in civil government should be toward the levels of government that are closer to the people served by the civil magistrates, not to the higher levels of civil government. This is the biblical deference to decentralization and localism that flows from a recognition of the need for the division of authority and diffusion of power.[1]

We know from history that human society began with one man and one woman. No civil government was needed until

---

1. The Bible does not provide a systematic model of what a biblical civil government looks like, but it does provide clear principles that, when followed, give us more restrictive parameters for acceptable civil government and social order than the scope of what is endorsed by Christians today.

family size expanded beyond what could be managed at a family level of government. As society grew, provision was made for civil magistrates to govern people groups.

In the tribal context of Israel we also see Moses learning how to structure government in terms of the model that was needed for judges as the society grew in size. His father-in-law saw him weighed down by hearing cases all day, so he advised Moses (Exodus 18:17-26):

> "What you are doing is not good. You and these people who come to you will only wear yourselves out. The work is too heavy for you; you cannot handle it alone. Listen now to me and I will give you some advice, and may God be with you. You must be the people's representative before God and bring their disputes to him. Teach them the decrees and laws, and show them the way to live and the duties they are to perform. But select capable men from all the people—men who fear God, trustworthy men who hate dishonest gain—and appoint them as officials over thousands, hundreds, fifties and tens. Have them serve as judges for the people at all times, but have them bring every difficult case to you; the simple cases they can decide themselves. That will make your load lighter, because they will share it with you. If you do this and God so commands, you will be able to stand the strain, and all these people will go home satisfied."

Moses listened to his father-in-law and did everything he said. He chose capable men from all Israel and made them leaders of the people, officials over thousands, hundreds, fifties and tens. They served as judges for the people at all times. The difficult cases they brought to Moses, but the simple ones they decided themselves.

In the Bible we see what appears to be quite a high level of comfort with meting out judgment and punishment for crime at a local community level, rather than requiring the highest level of government—the level most distant from the people—to deal with the most serious offences. Restitution was the preferred biblical way to deal with property crimes and some other offences. Local adjudication of such offences is far more practical than national adjudication, and much more likely to result in a just prosecution because it is in the community that you will find the witnesses, if there were any. Local adjudication also requires all parties to take responsibility by requiring offender, victim and neighbours to face each other and resolve the dispute together. This is not the place for a comprehensive defence of a biblical approach to restorative justice, but such a study is imperative for those serious about advancing a vision of social order that emphasizes personal responsibility, self-government, decentralization and localism.

On the other hand, the preference for imprisonment that we see in Canada and the rest of the world today, for all its other faults, is *also* very convenient for those with a preference for state-ism and national-level control over the country's criminal code. The modern philosophy of imprisonment implies that crimes are offences against the state, rather than against particular victims, and since the state is an impersonal institution, the best solution it can propose for crime is to warehouse people, administering their prosecution by way of a massive impersonal, bureaucratic system.

The point here is that in God's economy the state, though a necessary part of society, is only one of several legitimate players, and one that does not command the kind of deference we see given to it today. This has implications, as we shall see, for every part of life; for economic issues and justice issues as well as so-called "social" issues. The general public, however, will not accept this vision if no one articulates it, so until Christians return to this biblical orthodoxy and advocate a self-consistent Christian worldview and vision for society, instead of simply reacting to individual issues, we shall not win the hearts and minds of enough people to achieve victory in the current culture war.

In fact, not only are Christians *not* articulating a comprehensive worldview, but many of us are arguing self-contradictory positions, advancing Secularist economic ideas that, at a more foundational level, contradict the position we take in favour of marriage. Hence, we are not advancing a self-consistent, rational worldview; we are simply fighting for our various opinions on particular issues with no regard for whether the theological premises for one opinion conflict with the premises for our view on another issue. Such an approach is not intellectually credible, so it does not inspire confidence from others. It is not surprising, therefore, that people do not take us seriously.

Notwithstanding the spiritual dynamics involved in today's culture war between Christianity and Secular Humanism, Christians are not doing themselves any favours in the way they are trying to preserve the few areas of life for which they are motivated to fight. We need to devote some serious thought to cultivating a comprehensive, biblically based worldview—one that effectively fleshes out the reality of sphere sovereignty, one that gives primacy to the liberty principle that is rooted in authentic Christianity and that can inspire people broadly—even well beyond the church—to lend their support to a Christian vision and program for society.

We must now take some time to examine practical examples of what the growing encroachment of today's civil government looks like in terms of public policy, how this totalitarian vision is being imposed on Canadians, how this agenda contravenes the principle of sphere sovereignty and the separation of church and state, and what a Christian-based liberty-oriented alternative would look like. As Christians, we need to have a much better idea of the nature of the problem before us; and, as previously indicated, we need to work hard at cultivating a comprehensive alternative vision. Since the homosexual political movement has become the vanguard of the Secular Humanist agenda—the forefront of the modern campaign to impose a police state on Canada—it is necessary to spend some time examining this threat in particular.

The threat to liberty from homosexual activism

The push for homosexual "marriage" is not the first time the state has usurped the jurisdictional parameters of the church and the family in order to advance homosexual rights. The entire homosexual agenda is predicated on forcing a tyrannical state to take up residence in people's bedrooms. The legislation which governs most, if not all, legal and economic benefits that have been extended to homosexuals states that those applying for benefits outside of a marriage relationship have to be engaged in a sexual relationship. But such a criterion makes no sense if the civil government does not have the authority to confirm a person's claim that their relationship is sexual. "Will we now have conjugality police to ensure 'married' couples qualify?", asks eminent Canadian author and philosopher, Dr. William Gairdner.[2] He, of course, answers in the negative because homosexual activists know how outrageous this aspect of their strident socialist vision would be to most Canadians. But this illustrates yet another aspect of the huge con-game homosexual activists have played on Canadians. Because, as Dr. Gairdner points out: "Practically speaking, why does conjugality matter?" Having said that, though, we know that if two sisters living together applied for such benefits, they would be denied. This is what happened in Britain in a test case in 2006.[3] Homosexual activists will continue to have their cake and eat it too as long as nobody demands logic and intellectual integrity from them.

Another important aspect of the homosexual political agenda is the way the rhetoric about equal rights is used to obscure the true Secularist agenda of homosexual activists: affirmation, approval, dignity and endorsement—attitudes that are to be developed within the context of the family and the church, not the state.

One can find countless examples of comments from homosexuals and pro-homosexual politicians and journalists to substantiate the fact that what they want is affirmation, not simply equality. "... Heterosexuals acknowledged that same-sex couples mainly want just the respect, recognition and public affirmation that heterosexual couples have always taken for granted ..." wrote the London Free Press in an editorial supporting homosexual "marriage."[4]

2. "Mourning marriage," by Dr. William Gairdner. January 27, 2007.
   http://www.williamgairdner.com/journal/2007/1/27/mourning-marriage.html.
3. "Treat us like lesbians, say sisters in tax fight," by Joshua Rozenberg. *The Daily Telegraph*,
   September 13, 2006.
4. "Same-sex issue in MPs' hands." *London Free Press*, December 10, 2004.

"... and all Canadians will be able to congratulate themselves that gays and lesbians, once a stigmatized and sometimes ridiculed minority, have been given a constitutional right that recognizes their dignity as human beings," wrote the *Victoria Times-Colonist*.[5]

A mean-spirited assault against Saskatchewan marriage commissioner Orville Nichols provides dramatic testimony to this homosexualist mentality that the state has a legitimate function in affirming people and consoling a damaged self-image. Mr. Nichols refused to perform a marriage ceremony for two homosexuals. He referred them to another marriage commissioner and the "marriage" ceremony was preformed.[6] Nevertheless, these homosexuals decided to launch a "human rights" complaint against Mr. Nichols through the provincial kangaroo court, a.k.a. the Saskatchewan Human Rights Commission.

In explaining what was no doubt a big part of their rationale for pursuing the human rights complaint, one of the homosexuals, identified publicly as B.R., said his partner—who was 51 years old, chronologically anyway—"has gone through life under the radar, never having to deal with discrimination before. When it hit him, it hit him hard." The journalist, writing up the story, reported: "M.J. said he went through sleepless nights and anxiety following Mr. Nichols' refusal. Revealing himself as a gay man is something M.J. said he doesn't take lightly."

Why does such comment have any relevance to a story about a quasi-judicial process involving the use of the civil magistrate to punish someone? Do homosexual activists ever

---

5. "The right ruling on gay marriage." *Victoria Times Colonist*, December 12, 2004.
6. "Man cites religion for his refusal to wed gays," by Karen Brownlee, CanWest News Service. *National Post*, February 1, 2007.

move beyond adolescence? Why do heterosexual politicians tolerate these feigned expressions of hurt feelings?[7] It's time to draw a line in the sand and to tell homosexualists to join the adult population and to "get over it" when somebody doesn't give them the affirmation that they desire regarding their sexual proclivities and their personal, deeply held beliefs that they should self-identify primarily on the basis of those sexual practises. Politicians, however, probably won't do this until there is a greater general recognition that the state has no business playing the role of parents in people's lives.

The idea that the state has a legitimate role to play towards these goals of affirmation and personal respect is very much consistent with Secularism's socialistic political theory, which sees all of life, including the church and its function, subsumed under the authority of the state. Christian political theory, however, gives the state no role in the pursuit of such goals. Concern over affirmation and approval, self-image and personal development involve the character you develop (or do not develop) as you grow up in your family. They are also cultivated with the help of friends and the support system that people build around themselves in their communities and informal relations, centred, for Christians, in their church life. Therefore, when people demand affirmation and approval from the state, they are demanding that the state step outside its biblically sanctioned sphere of authority to interpose itself onto the jurisdictions of the family and the church.

7. The vindictive and political nature of these "human rights" complaints is sometimes transparent, as in this case. More fair-minded people have dismissed concerns about a direct clash between homosexual rights and religious freedom in cases involving marriage, arguing, "Why would homosexuals want someone who opposes their rights performing their marriage ceremony?" ("Marriage commissioners have rights, too," by Tom Broadbeck. *The Winnipeg Sun*, October 8, 2006) Why indeed! Such is the vindictive and totalitarian spirit that runs through much of homosexual activism. M.J. left a wife and children to pursue his homosexual impulses. What serious individual is going to offer this 51-year-old any sympathy for supposedly feeling hurt by Mr. Nichols' "discrimination"?

In fact, self-government and the cultivation of good character is the primary place where questions of affirmation and approval are resolved. People who feel the need for these expressions from an external source, worse yet from the civil government, are individuals who have failed to cultivate the kind of character that makes self-government possible. They are demanding from the state something that ultimately only God can give them. But once people have rejected God and self-government, where else can they turn? In this respect, we see the growth of state-ism as evidence of the decline in the influence of Christianity in our culture.

Ultimately, it is when a person sees the state as his "Daddy"—a view consistent with the idea of the state as all-encompassing, even taking on the familial roles of husbands and fathers—that he needs the kind of affirmation from the civil magistrate that is demanded by homosexual activists. This preoccupation reinforces social theory which suggests that homosexuality can almost always be traced back to dysfunctional, if not abusive, relationships with a man's father. (Of course, what homosexual activists are also after is the preferential treatment that naturally comes with affirmation, preferential treatment that, by its very nature, makes a mockery of homosexualist claims that all they want is equality.)

One of the most shocking examples of this radical imposition of the modern Secularist state into the realms of the church and the family is found in the decision by the B.C. Court of Appeal (cited earlier) in a case against B.C. public school teacher and counselling psychologist Chris Kempling. The British Columbia College of Teachers (BCCT) inquisition against this Christian teacher is one of the most vicious examples to date of the passionate hatred Canadian homosexual activists have towards anyone who criticizes homosexuality. Siding with these activists, and articulating the Secular state's belief in its right to act in the role of clergy and parents, the Appeal court judge ruled:

> In my view, it is only when these statements are made in disregard of an individual's inherent dignity that they become [discriminatory]. To hold an individual in contempt or to judge them, in the words of Abella J.A., as she then was, in *R. v. Carmen M.* (1995), 23 O.R. (3d) 629 at 633, "based not on their actual individual capacities, but on stereotypical characteristics ascribed to them because they are attributed to the group of which the individuals are a member," is to treat that individual in a manner which is not consonant with their inherent dignity.

Even if that were the case, so what? What business is it of the civil magistrate to be concerned about arbitrating conflicts based on human dignity? The very notion is inherently tyrannical. It requires a radical degree of intervention by the state, as blunt and oppressive an instrument as it is, in areas of life that truly free individuals once felt confident in their own ability to arbitrate. To welcome the state into this jurisdiction is to surrender a massive scope of individual liberty, including freedom of speech (the primary concern in the Kempling case), as it came to us—and the West—by way of the Christian worldview. This interest by the state in arbitrating matters of human dignity reveals the radical antithesis between the liberty principle that is fundamental to authentic Christianity and the agenda of tyranny that is fundamental to Secularism.

Mr. Kempling took his case all the way to the Supreme Court of Canada, losing at each stage with the Supreme Court deciding not to hear the case. The intellectual puerility of Canada's judges and the cabal of lawyers from which they are selected are humiliating to any thoughtful Canadian. That the Supremes did not see a principle of fundamental liberty in this case that was important enough to examine, boggles the mind.

Another powerful example of Secularism's link between governmental tyranny and a hatred for the family is the ACLU, probably the most aggressive champion of Secular Humanism in North America today. As a champion of Secularism, the ACLU is driven by the vision of Communism. This is not well known because the leadership of the organisation knows that Communism is filthy and barbaric to many Americans. Yet we cannot deny ACLU founder Roger Baldwin's commitment to Socialism: "I am for socialism, disarmament, and ultimately for abolishing the state itself as an instrument of violence and compulsion. I seek social ownership of property, the abolition of the propertied class, and sole control by those who produce wealth. Communism is the goal."[8] And we read elsewhere that, "The American Civil Liberties Union is Roger Baldwin."[9] Those who understand philosophy recognise this spirit in the ACLU still today, especially in the organisation's fanatical law-breaking, civil disobedience strategy to force homosexual "marriage" onto Americans.[10] For example, "When [San Francisco] Mayor Newsom made his decision to openly defy state law, the ACLU was standing right beside him. Tamara Lange, an ACLU staff attorney, said, 'We are

---

8. Peggy Lamson, *Roger Baldwin: Founder of the American Civil Liberties Union: A Portrait* (Boston: Houghton-Mifflin, 1976), p. 192, as cited in Alan Sears and Craig Osten, The ACLU vs. America (Nashville, Tennessee: Broadman & Holdman, 2005), p. 7

9. William Donohue, *The Politics of the American Civil Liberties Union*, (New Brunswick, NJ: Transaction Publishers, 1985), p. 45.

10. Alan Sears and Craig Osten, *The ACLU vs. America* (Nashville, Tennessee: Broadman & Holdman, 2005), pp. 34ff.

eager to take on this historic opportunity to end marriage discrimination in California'."[11]

The recent decision by Britain's homosexual-hijacked Labour government to require Christians, specifically Catholic adoption agencies, to facilitate the adoption of children by homosexual couples is another example of use of homosexual activism to expand the power of the state over what should be private spheres of life, including the family, religious convictions and the human conscience.[12] Colin Hart, director of the Christian Institute, a charity which seeks to promote Christianity in Britain, condemned British Prime Minister Tony Blair's statement that no exceptions to the new law would be granted to Catholic adoption agencies, asserting accurately that "the government is putting up a sign over the U.K. saying, 'Christians are not welcome here.'"[13]

The threat, however, is not fundamentally from homosexuality but, rather, from the further encroachment of the civil government into what should be treated as the private sphere of the family. This move flows out of a demagogic spirit. It is another example of how the size and degree of interference of the civil government increases with the erosion of the traditional family. It reflects a vision of social order that is antithetical to the Christian vision for culture and civil society. A culture of intact families would not require—or tolerate— this kind of fascistic interference in the nation's family life. Of course, the foundation for this recent development was built some years earlier with the civil government establishing its

11. "Legal Groups Say Denial of Marriage Licenses Violates State Constitution," ACLU press release, March 12, 2004. http://www.aclu.org/news/newsprint.cfm?ID=15254&c=101.
12. "Davis backs Catholics in gay adoption row as the pressure mounts on Cameron," by Graeme Wilson. *The Daily Telegraph*, January 29, 2007.
13. Church loses battle to opt out of gay adoption," by George Jones. *National Post*, January 30, 2007.

authority over the adoption process. No doubt, Christians didn't put up the kind of fight they should have at the time. So we reap what we sow. It will be a long, uphill battle for Christians to reclaim under the jurisdiction of family government with the support of the Church, the primary responsibility for facilitating the adoption of children. Christians in Canada and other countries should note well what has just taken place in Great Britain.

Researchers link tyranny and homosexual "marriage"

The examples already cited paint a horrific picture of the oppressive and tyrannical nature of homosexual activism, but the Secularist agenda to redefine marriage may well be worse. The police state mentality that drives Secularism is made transparent in homosexual activists' anti-marriage agenda. Daniel Cere, a professor at McGill University in Montreal, Quebec does a vital job of articulating the diabolical nature of this anti-marriage ideology as the principal investigator for a report prepared for the Council on Family Law. The Council on Family Law is a group that is jointly sponsored by the Institute for American Values, the Institute for Marriage and Public Policy and the Institute for the Study of Marriage, Law and Culture.

In his 2005 report for the Council[14], Professor Cere,[15] writes:

Ironically, the consequence of disestablishment [the name given to the perspective that the state should

14. The report, published in 2005, is entitled, "The Future of Family Law: Law and the Marriage Crisis in North America". Pages 30-32.
15. Daniel Cere is also the co-editor of the highly acclaimed book *Divorcing Marriage: Unveiling the Dangers in Canada's New Social Experiment*. Editors: Daniel Cere and Douglas Farrow. Published by McGill-Queen's University Press, 2004.

get out of the marriage business—"the separation of marriage and state"] is not likely to be greater individual freedom, but rather more intense and far-reaching state regulation of formerly private relations. Married people generally regulate their family affairs without direct government interference, except in cases of criminality or violence. By comparison, the state routinely tells divorced and unmarried parents when they can see their kids and how much child support to pay, and often intervenes in thorny disagreements such as what school the child will attend, or what religion he or she will be raised in, or if a parent is allowed to relocate. Outside of marriage, the state is necessarily drawn into greater and more intrusive regulation of family life. Because sex between men and women continues to produce children, and because women raising children alone are economically and socially disadvantaged, governments will continually wrestle with expensive and intrusive efforts to protect children born outside of marital unions.

… If conjugal relationships "vary widely and almost infinitely," then virtually any caring or sharing close relationship is arguably worthy of state recognition and social support. Such a move appears to set the stage for a vast extension of the rule of law into the sphere of intimate relations, including legal recognition of multiple close relationships.

Professor Cere is not the only expert making this point. Jennifer Roback Morse includes a devastating critique of how homosexual "marriage" helps drive a stake through the heart of freedom and equality, simultaneously expanding and strengthening the power of the state over people's lives in her 2005 report, "Deconstructing Marriage: Less Freedom; More Inequality."[16]

Seana Sugrue, D.C.L., a Canadian now teaching in Florida, in the Department of Politics at Ave Maria University, conveyed the same message to parliamentarians in Ottawa in the spring of 2006. The paper on which she based her remarks to Canada's federal politicians was published in the Institute of Marriage and Family Canada's May 2006 *Report*.[17]

In an article which focused on the threat that homosexual "marriage" poses to children,[18] Professor Sugrue also discusses the state-ist implications of abandoning marriage and natural parenthood:

There are a number of serious ethical problems with the attempt to eradicate, by law, the significance of a

16. "Deconstructing Marriage: Less Freedom; More Inequality," by Jennifer Roback Morse. *IMFC Review*, Fall/Winter 2005. Pp. 25-27.
17. "Canadian Marriage Policy: A Tragedy for Children," by Seana Sugrue. "Report," May 31, 2006. http://www.imfcanada.org/Default.aspx?go=article&aid=91&tid=8.
18. Prof. Sugrue classifies homosexual "marriage" as a form of "companionate" marriage, the increasingly popular notion within Canada's political and legal establishment that "marriage is ... first and foremost about the companionate and emotional needs of consenting adults. For this reason, it is contended that the rules governing marriage laws ought to be purged of any expectation that children are begotten from adult sexual unions. Moreover, there ought to be no expectation that children ought to be raised by their mother and father within the institution of marriage." In other words, homosexual "marriage" is but a symptom of a more comprehensive social revolution in which childish and self-absorbed adults are redefining fundamental social norms, threatening individual liberty and Canada's social order in the process. At the point where Prof. Sugrue defined companionate marriage in her article, she provided the following footnote: "Marriage, from the point of view of the secular state authority," opined the Law Commission of Canada, "is a means of facilitating in an orderly fashion the voluntary assumption of mutual rights and obligations by adults committed to each other's well-being." See Law Commission of Canada. (2001). The Legal Organization of Personal Relationships [Electronic version]. "Beyond Conjugality: Recognizing and Supporting Close Personal Relationships." Retrieved from http://www.lcc.gc.ca/about/conjugality_toc-en.asp.

mother and a father to a child, as well as marriage as the institution within which a mother and a father are expected to procreate and rear their children.

... The ethical issue that arises from the attempt to redefine marriage as serving the needs of adults, not children, is that it invites, over time, greater state intrusions into family life. This is necessitated by the fact that the state must increasingly intervene into the realm of the family to determine who owes obligations to whom. Where marriage is the union of one man and one woman who are responsible for the rearing of their begotten children and for one another, the state generally need not intervene to determine to whom children within such unions belong. The state's role is primarily a supportive one of recognizing what the parents, and society at large, take to be obligatory because of established familial relations. Once it can no longer be assumed that children belong to a mother and a father, where it is possible for children to be claimed by two mothers, or two fathers, or some other combination, then it is imperative for the state to intervene to settle the question of belonging and of responsibility.

Dr. Allan Carlson, president of The Howard Center for Family, Religion and Society, has also discussed the inherently socialistic nature of homosexual "marriage," as well as other alternatives to the historic and Christian teaching on marriage and the family. At a symposium in September 2006, called "What's The Harm? How Legalizing Same-Sex Marriage Will Harm Society, Families, Adults, Children and Marriage," he said: "Granting certain claims to cohabitating gays and lesbians in 1987 and extending 'registered partnerships' to the same in

1995 were part of this historic transition – from the family as an autonomous institution focused on the bearing and rearing of children to the 'new family,' socialist in form, understood as an ever-changing network of relationships dependent on the state."[19]

According to a Howard Center press release on Dr. Carlson's symposium comments, he also "shows how the introduction of registered partnerships in Scandinavia was part of a much broader ideological project designed to alter fundamentally, and weaken, the legal institution of marriage. Behind this drive is a unique combination of conventional socialism, feminism and neo-Malthusianism which seeks to substitute the state for the family."[20]

Professor Cere provides more evidence of the totalitarian nature of Secular Humanism's anti-marriage agenda, with his comments on *Principles of the Law of Family Dissolution*, an anti-family report produced by the American Law Institute. Professor Cere writes, in reference to the parenthood implications of redefining marriage out of adult relationships: "Almost as an afterthought, the ALI's new close relationship marital regime transforms parenthood into a domain created by the state."[21] He writes earlier: "Parenthood [in ALI's modeling] becomes a flexible legal category, with the courts—rather than the child's existing parents—determining when a person has devoted enough care and attention to an unrelated child to acquire parental rights."[22]

19. "Allan Carlson addresses same-sex marriage symposium, 'What's the harm,' at BYU Law School," Press release, The Howard Center for Family, Religion and Society, September 15, 2006.
20. Ibid.
21. "Future of Family Law: Law and the Marriage Crisis in North America," A Report from the Council on Family Law, Dan Cere, Principal Investigator. Institute for American Values, 2005. p. 37.
22. Ibid, p. 36.

The totalitarian nature of homosexual "marriage" is not surprising in light of the tyrannical sympathies of those advocating it. Professor Cere cites one such individual in "The Future of Family Law": "Those determined to alter the public meaning of marriage admonish us to shelve such questions [about "a vast extension of the rule of law into the sphere of intimate relations"]. A Canadian human rights lawyer insists that problematic concerns about where new legal changes might lead need 'not be decided at this point.' The immediate and pressing legal challenge is to redefine marriage in order to include same-sex couples. Raising the problem of future legal implications 'merely complicates an already thorny issue'."[23]

The anti-rationality of this lawyer's position is astonishing. The man lacks the courage and intellectual integrity to engage in debate over the legitimacy of his position. He is a demagogue: he wants to impose his ideology on people without being able to give a rational, satisfactory and comprehensive defence for his position. This lawyer – and those like him – is a dangerous threat to the survival in Canada of democratic ideals such as individual liberty and equality before the law.

Having summarized several researchers' comments on the state-ist nature of the agenda to abolish marriage, Jennifer Morse's thorough comments on the multiple sociological dynamics at play deserve extensive citation here[24]:

> ... However, abolishing organic marriage will reduce both freedom and equality. Freedom will be reduced

23. P. 32 of "The Future of Family Law" – and the citation in that report is: Julius Grey, "Equality Rights Versus the right to Marriage: Toward the Path of Canadian Compromise." *Policy Options*, October, 2003: 33.
24. "Deconstructing Marriage: Less Freedom; More Inequality," by Jennifer Roback Morse. *IMFC Review*, Fall/Winter 2005. Pp. 26-27.

because both the taxation and regulatory power of the state will expand. Equality will be harmed because some types of family structures create systematically better life chances for children than others. Even massive investments by the state are unlikely to fully equalize the life chances of children from different types of families.

Some kinds of families objectively function better than others. The children of unmarried or divorced parents are more likely than other children to have emotional, behavioural and health problems. As these children become old enough to go to school, they have lowered school achievement, poor school attendance, and discipline problems. As these children mature, they are more likely to get into trouble with the law, commit crimes, abuse drugs, and end up in jail.[25]

These systematic differences between the children of married parents and other children have consequences for both equality and for freedom. The parents may be treated "equally" by the state in the sense that the state attempts to be impartial among family forms. But the life chances of the children are not equal.[26] The children of unmarried parents are more likely to be poor and less likely to go to college. These kinds of differences persist over the lifetime. The state can respond to this situation in one of two ways. The state may take the "leave us alone" attitude to its logical conclusion.

25. In general, see Doherty, W., et al. (2002). "Why marriage matters: Twenty-one conclusions from the social sciences." New York: Institute for American Values. Or Fagan, P.F., & Rector, R. (2000, June 5). "The effects of divorce on America." Washington, D.C.: The Heritage Foundation Backgrounder, No. 1373.

26. David Blankenhorn (1995) argues that having married parents or not is creating the new and most long-lasting forms of inequality. See his "Fatherless America: Confronting our most urgent social problem." New York: Basic Books.

The parents have made these life-style decisions; the state will not interfere with the consequences of those decisions. This government policy simply allows the income inequality among the children to persist.

In today's political climate, this is not a very likely or very stable policy outcome. The more likely alternative government response is that the state will pump resources into the alternative families, to try and offset some of the disadvantages the children face. Direct income support for the children of unmarried parents is only the tip of the iceberg, because the costs are more than purely private costs to the mother and father. The costs of health care, schooling, and mental health care are not entirely private in modern society. A child who can not behave in school is a cost to the local school district as well as to all the other children in the classroom. A seriously depressed person, or a substance dependent person, is likely to make demands on the public health sector. If the child ends up in the criminal justice system, as the children of unmarried parents are significantly more likely to do, they will be a significant cost to the state. ...

This tension between freedom and equality for adults and freedom and equality for children is not confined to the fiscal sphere of government. The great irony of family law is this: in the name of personal privacy, we have weakened the social norms that govern family life. When families dissolve, we allow the state to intervene in the most personal areas of family life. Let me describe a hypothetical example that illustrates the point.

A man and woman have a child. The mother and father have no permanent relationship to each other, and no desire to form one. When the relationship ceases to function to their satisfaction, it dissolves. The mother sues the father for child support.

The couple argues through the court system over how much he should pay. The woman wants him to pay more than he wants to pay. The court ultimately orders him to pay a particular amount. He insists on continuing visitation rights with his child. She resists. They argue in court, and finally settle on a periodic visitation schedule to which he is entitled.

The agreement works smoothly at first. Then the parents quarrel. At visitation time, the mother is not home. He calls and leaves a nasty message on the answering machine. They quarrel some more. She says his behaviour is not appropriate. He smokes too much, and over-indulges the child in sweets. She says the child, who is now a toddler, is impossible to deal with after visits. He quits paying child support. The court garnishes his wages to force him to pay. He goes to court to try to get his visitation agreement honoured. The court appoints a mediator to help the couple work out a solution. The mother announces that she plans to move. He goes to court and gets a temporary order to restrain her from moving. She invents a charge of child abuse and gets a restraining order forbidding him from seeing the child.

Say what you like about this sort of case. You may think this is the best mere mortals can do. You may think this contentiousness is the necessary price people pay for their adult independence. You may blame the mother or the father or both. Or perhaps you think this is a nightmare for both adults as well as for children. But on one point we can all agree: this is not a free society in which the state honours people's privacy. Agents of the government actively inquire into, pass judgments upon and intervene in the most intimate details of this couple's life.

The state solicitude for the mother and her child is a direct result of father absence. Without a father's assistance, this woman and her child are more likely to become dependents of the state. The state believes, quite reasonably, that it is more cost-effective to help the mother extract assistance from the father, than to provide taxpayer-funded financial assistance. Aggressive programs for tracking down "dead-beat dads," become a substitute for providing direct payments through the welfare system as conventionally understood ...

We all recognize that a free market needs a culture of law-abidingness, promise-keeping and respect for contracts. Similarly, a free society needs a culture that supports and sustains marriage as the normative institution for the begetting, bearing and rearing of children. A culture full of people who violate their contracts at every possible opportunity can not be held together by legal institutions, as the experience of post-communist Russia plainly shows. Likewise, a society full of people who treat sex as a purely recreational activity, a child as a consumer good, and marriage as a glorified roommate relationship, will not be able to resist the pressures for a vast social assistance state, and for an overbearing family court system. The state will irresistibly be drawn into parental quarrels and into providing a variety of services for the well-being of the children.

What these and other researchers have shown is that this trend toward state-ism by way of the abandonment of marriage and natural or biological parenthood has been at work for decades now through such reforms as relaxing divorce legislation, as with "no-fault" divorce, the toleration of common-law arrangements and treating non-marital arrangements as equivalent to marriage in public policy. Homosexual "marriage" is yet another step in this natural socialistic progression from intact families towards the tyranny of state-ism. Dr. Gairdner's explanation of this point is important to note here:[27]

> Citizens must beware the insidious reputation of the modern state in relation to the special role, influence, and survival of the natural family. Empires, principalities, and states, however defined, have always had one thing in common: a natural antipathy to any other human organization or association within their jurisdiction that competes with the state for the loyalty of citizens. Principal among such associations have been religion and the family, the two social entities—the first spiritual, the second biological—to which people have always given a private allegiance more powerful than their public feeling for country or rulers.

This sort of tension was visible in ancient Rome, where the law of the family and the law of mighty

---

27. "Mourning marriage," by Dr. William Gairdner. January 27, 2007.
   http://www.williamgairdner.com/journal/2007/1/27/mourning-marriage.html.

Rome itself were often in conflict, the state as often giving way. Indeed, in many European nations, even today, no monarch or ruler, no matter how absolute the power has ever had the unfettered or capricious right to enter a private home without permission of the family. But the most insidious incursions of state power into family relations and property rights have been felt since the advent of the mighty tax-harvesting social-welfare states of modern times, many of which have declared an open or covert war against the private family, seeing it as a cradle of social privilege and inequality. Accordingly, they have specifically sought to weaken the natural biological bonds of marriage as the family's foundation. Marx and Engels based much of their disastrous communist social program on a deep distrust of the private family. That was socialism with machine guns. But the softer social-welfare states that arose in the 20th century—of which Sweden and Canada are the most ideologically fervent examples— have at their foundation the very same animus against the family and indeed against all biologically-based distinctions, privileges, or differences between citizens that might pose a threat to the only claim of such states to a quasi-moral authority: the guarantee of citizen equality in all things. Aware as they are that the family has a deep and powerful blood-grip on its members for life, such states take the softer, less visible approach. They weaken the grip of the family and its privileges not by eliminating the latter, but rather by dissolving their unique value and prestige by removing all qualifications for receiving them; that is, by showering them without discrimination on everyone alike. Just so, a deeply biologically-rooted institution such as marriage can be gradually transformed into yet another vehicle for political equalization. For this, citizens who have not seen what is really at work bow down and give thanks to the state.

And North America's "sex activists" aren't finished yet. "After a decade of fighting for same-sex 'marriage,' some homosexual activists are breaking their silence to say it's time to fight for benefits for all kinds of relationships," reported *The Washington Times* in August 2006.[28] "Families and relationships 'know no borders and will never slot narrowly into a single existing template,' several activists said in a statement issued last month called 'Beyond Marriage: A New Strategic Vision For All Our Families and Relationships.' Because marriage is 'not the only worthy form of family or relationship,' it 'should not be legally or economically privileged above others,' according to the statement, which was signed by 270 homosexual rights activists and heterosexual allies, such as Princeton University professor Cornel West and feminist icon Gloria Steinem." Tyranny is an addictive tonic to these sex activists, driven, as they are, by their devotion to Secularist ideology.

Understanding the scope of the problem

All this evidence points to the real problem Canada faces today: the encroachment of the state into the affairs of the family and the church—not the other way around. Looking at the current controversy over the attempt to redefine marriage, we can see that the real reason for the outcry against the participation of church leaders in the debate over homosexual "marriage" is not a concern over the church interfering in the legitimate jurisdiction of the state. Rather, it is the defensive

28. "Gays expand battlefield," by Cheryl Wetzstein. *The Washington Times*, August 9, 2006.
    http://www.washingtontimes.com/culture/20060808-104605-1600r.htm.

133

reaction of vested interests attempting to protect their illegitimate positions of power and authority against people (e.g. clergy and parents) who are—finally—seeking to regain control over their legitimate sphere of authority. This is not to say that clergy and families realize that this is what they are doing. Hopefully this book will go some way to educating Canadians that this is, indeed, what they ought to be doing— that way they can pursue this goal with more confidence and clarity of thought.

This is important because the problem with the state overstepping its lawful parameters for action did not begin with the homosexual political movement and it is not exclusive to it. Secular Humanism has been pushing this anti-Christian agenda for several decades already, most significantly with the establishment of the social welfare state. So, if Christians are serious about regaining control over the definition of marriage, then they are going to have to take back a lot more than marriage. We are in a culture war, not a single-issue war and it is not clear yet that a sufficient number of Christians understand the significance of this reality. This situation needs to change.

The fact that there has been so little resistance to homosexual political demands over the past decade or more indicates that the philosophical basis for their agenda resonates broadly with the general public—or at the very least, does not cause such alarm among people as to generate a groundswell of broad-based opposition. Christians need to recognise this comprehensive nature of the battle between Christianity and Secularism so that they can better understand the battle they are in; because fighting for marriage alone, while leaving the intellectual pillars of Secularism in place, is a losing battle—

as is indicated by the defeat social conservatives have faced thus far in this conflict.

Those who oppose the advancement of "homosexual rights" talk about the threat posed to the family; but the homosexual political movement is only one of many attacks launched against the Canadian family ever since the introduction of the social welfare state—and the social welfare state mentality— into Canadian political governance. In order to position itself as the final authority over all of life, Secularism has had progressively to undermine respect for, and the authority of, church government, family government and self-government. This battle has been taking place for decades with Christians, for the most part, seemingly unaware of the big picture and the long-term agenda of their Secularist enemies (judging by their lack of engagement to combat this Secularist onslaught).

True, opposition to some of these attacks has existed to one degree or another, particularly on issues such as child care, parental discipline of children and sex education. In other areas, however, distinctly Christian opposition has been muted, such as in opposition to high taxes, gun control, assaults on property rights and the regulatory fanaticism that governs every area of Canadian life from health supplements to building codes, from environmental protection to a host of other areas where the state supposedly needs to intervene in our private decisions for the sake of health and safety.

Christianity is a worldview; it requires consistent living across all aspects of life. One cannot live for long in one area of life under the direction of principles that are contradictory to the principles that govern how we behave in another aspect of our lives. If Christians helped to open the door to homosexual activism, including the demand for same-sex "marriage," by endorsing a more fundamental theological principle that provides a logical justification for that agenda, then we are responsible before God and man to close that philosophical door again—even if the process proves to be painful, requiring a rethinking of our beliefs and values over a wide spectrum of issues.

Separation of state and church—Reclaiming ground for the church and the family

As we have noted, today the call for the separation of church and state is coming from Secularists who claim to want the church to stay out of the affairs of the state; or more accurately, for Christians to avoid trying to impose their moral standards on others.

How many people remember hearing this cry come up from Secular Humanists when the state was increasing its influence in society by increasingly encroaching on the rightful jurisdictions of the church and the family? If Secular Humanists were committed as a matter of principle to "sphere sovereignty," you would have heard all kinds of objections since the beginning of the social welfare agenda several decades go. But you did not—because Secular Humanists support political absolutism, with control by the civil magistrate over all of life. Secularists do not support sphere sovereignty; they are outraged when the church, the family and individuals try to re-assert their governmental authority over areas granted to them by God, over against the encroachment of the state that has been taking place over the past generation or more.

It would be wrong to blame Secular Humanists alone for this situation because, as indicated above, there was much Christian support for (or at the very least, acquiescence in) this agenda of tyranny and political idolatry. Sadly, socialism is seductive because it appeals to concerns and desires that exist among all people, including Christians. The aspirations and rhetoric of socialism are largely admirable. Unfortunately, however, the methodology of socialism is political centralism because the theology of socialism is atheism and the religion of socialism is idolatrous state-worship. That is why socialism has failed everywhere that it has been tried—often to the great misery and harm of many people—because its methodology does not conform to reality as God has created it.

The progressive nature of the advancement of paternalistic and maternalistic government was slow enough that it drew many, if not most, Christians into its seductive grip. Even now, it is probably safe to say that most Canadian Christians do not appreciate the intricate relationship in a coherent worldview between social welfare, the definition of marriage, tax rates, gun control and abortion. Far more of them are motivated to fight the battles over marriage, abortion, gambling and pornography—so-called "social conservative" issues—than are willing to fight for property rights, deregulation of the media, lower taxes and gun ownership rights. We hone in on particular battles without recognizing how they fit into the big picture. We hope to stop a particular advancement of Secularism without realizing that we have accepted many earlier advances of Secularism, thereby showing ourselves to be inconsistent and irrational—abandoning the intellectual and theological foundations necessary to win the battles on issues such as abortion and the definition of marriage.

Big picture thinking in this respect requires recognizing that God has indeed established separate spheres of jurisdictional function for the family, the church and the state; and growing in our understanding of what responsibilities fall under the governance of each authority, as well as how self-government fills out the complete picture. For example, the fact that it is good to help the poor does not justify any and all means to help the poor. Christianity is supposed to abhor the ethic of "the end justifies the means."

Is coercively extracted taxation to redistribute income to the poor a biblically sanctioned means for helping the poor? A thorough debate on this point will have to wait for another time, but frankly, the answer is no. We should be able to say that just as quickly as we repudiate the notion that the church has the right to execute people simply because the Bible sanctions capital punishment. A correct understanding of sphere sovereignty is fundamental to a correct understanding of God's moral demands in this world, including his infallible directives as to how we should order human society.

In the early years of the social welfare state, many people—including many well-meaning Christians—thought that allowing the state to help people in need through such policies as social welfare, rent subsidies, unemployment insurance, social security, "free" healthcare, "free" education and childcare subsidies, etc., would be a good way to assist parents. Instead, honest people today are forced to acknowledge that the sinfulness of the sinful nature is far worse than most of us want to believe. Hence, we have seen all sorts of abuses of government programs. Parents abandon their responsibility to educate their children to the state instead of seeing themselves as participants with teachers. Rights-based ideology prevents bureaucrats from distinguishing between the deserving and undeserving poor, so the biblical principle of not feeding a man who can work but refuses to do so cannot be applied in the distribution of social welfare funds. Institutionalized welfare is dehumanizing, less accountable than family, church and community based aid, and tends to subsidize the deviant behaviour (such as extra-marital sex) that resulted in poverty in the first place (e.g., by way of pregnancy and single-parenthood as a consequence of extra-marital sex).

One necessary way of looking at the social welfare state is to see it as the illegitimate encroachment of the state into the divinely-mandated sphere of family governance. It is the responsibility of men, as husbands and fathers, to provide for their families. Economic life essentially flows out of the family. Small business is known to be the driving force of a vibrant economy. Small businesses used more often than not to be of the "father and son" variety. This does not have to be the case, but this observation points to the centrality of the local, community, family context for the personal development and education[29] that are among the best predictors for productive economic activity among adults.

To put it another way, private property rights and a vibrant, competitive, entrepreneurial, unregulated free enterprise economic model flows out of a Christian ethic, whereas Secular Humanism imposes an ever-increasing level of suffocating and pernicious regulations on economic activity, regulations that increasingly originate in the context of

---

29. We are seeing renewed interest in the concept of apprenticeship today with a broader cross-section of the business world trying to make apprenticeships available. Apprenticeship is no longer seen as simply a rural, pre-industrial or blue-collar concept. The educative superiority of this God-ordained methodology is clearly recognized by those who know how to identify success. It reflects an assault on the centralist, socialist concept of education, although many people have yet to realize this fact.

politicized "science" and the emotional aftermath of isolated tragic incidences, instead of on the basis of reasoned cost-benefit analyses. An unsupervised child squeezes through the bars of a high-rise apartment's balcony and falls to her death. The next thing you know, the civil government is requiring all apartment building owners to replace open-style balcony enclosures with solid panels—and you can only find three people in the entire province of Ontario willing to condemn this ridiculous, politically motivated and socialistic means to the end of protecting children who are permitted by their parents and guardians to play on high-rise balconies. There is barely any resistance today to Secularist ideology. Those who oppose it on particulars are generally afraid to voice their concerns because, lacking an underlying coherent worldview and philosophical basis for their opposition, they know their arguments will not withstand scrutiny. That is where Christians find themselves today in the culture war that we are fighting.

The social welfare state has also ripped the heart out of motherhood. Intact families are not treated as superior to broken and incomplete families in public policy – even though we have much solid research showing this to be the case in terms of child outcomes.[30] Governments appeal to spurious research to argue that the sooner that parents give up their children to "professionals" and institutional care, the better for the child's long-term development. They take our tax dollars to pay for this care for those families who accept the government's programs. The high tax burden in general imposes excessive pressures on families, driving many families to decide they need

---

30. E.g., "Make him buy the cow," by Barbara Kay. National Post, October 5, 2005; "Relationships Among Involvement, Attachment, and Behavioral Problems in Adolescence: Examining Father's Influence," by Susan K. Williams and F. Donald Kelly. Journal of Early Adolescence, 25 [2005]: 168-196; "Incarcerated Drug-Abusing Mothers: Their Characteristics and Vulnerability," by Thomas E. Hanlon et al. The American Journal of Drug and Alcohol Abuse, 1 [2005]: 59-77.

a second income with the wife's salary usually going entirely
to the government to cover the family's tax bill. Politicians and
bureaucrats condemn normal childrearing—including the use
of spanking—treating parents as abusers when they resort to
corporal punishment.[31] Governments look the other way when
"children's aid" agents intimidate, threaten and harass parents.
Governments also frown on parents who want to educate their
own children at home.[32]

Much of the risk to the freedoms of religion, conscience and
assembly in Canada today is due to attempts by an absolutist
Secular Humanist state to micromanage the lives of individual
Canadians. Today's Secular Humanist governments are not
interested in simply being agents of justice; they also want to
be agents of mercy. This role requires micro-managing and
aggressive intervention because this role requires imitating
the role of parents, spouses, friends and family. Yet, in the
same way that you might damage your window if you use
a sledgehammer to kill a mosquito, or might wreck your
house if you use an explosive devise to scare that raccoon
out of your basement, using the massive and blunt tool of the
state to administer charity is, at best, grossly inefficient; and,
at worst, horribly destructive. We can see these results all
around us today in the broken lives, the dysfunctional medical
system, the anarchy in our schools, and the numerous other
"social" problems we face in Canada today. These problems
are systemic, inherent in the very idea of the government
participating in these functions. These problems are due to

31. E.g., "Committee on Rights of Child Concludes Thirty-Fourth Session." UN Committee on
    the Rights of Child press release. October 3, 2003; "Ontario man sentenced to one year
    probation for spanking son," LifeSite Daily News, May 21, 2003.
32. Even in supposedly conservative Alberta, home schoolers have only just won a long
    drawn-out battle against greater regulations that the province wanted to impose on them.
    Cf. "Alberta Home Education Regulation," HSLDA Canada E-Report, Vol. 6 No. 10,
    August 1, 2006.

the fact that attempts to give the state a function in charity are attempts to work against God-ordained reality, including God's plan for the legitimate function of the state. Tweaking the system will not solve these problems, yet that is the approach all accepted "experts" use today in attempts to find solutions to Canada's social problems.

Conservative columnist and the editor of National Review Online, Jonah Goldberg, has said it well in his Sept. 23, 2005 column[33]:

> ... Both compassionate conservatism and welfare-state liberalism alike are uncompassionate. Inheriting from the neocons a basic philosophical comfort with the concept of the welfare state, compassionate conservatism— which also goes by 'big government conservatism'— sees no pressing need to pare government down to its core functions. Traditional conservatism, on the other hand, considers a lean government essential to the task of fulfilling its core responsibilities. ... Ultimately, this is the core problem with all ideologies that try to make government an extension of the family. Welfare-state liberalism wants the government to act like your mommy. Compassionate conservatives want the state to be your daddy. The problem: Government cannot love you, nor should it try. Love empowers us to do some things government must never have the power to do and other things the government can almost never do well.

More people by far "fall through the cracks" of state-initiated social welfare programs than suffer in the face of family-, church- and community-based charitable initiatives. No Christian needs to be concerned that advocating for the repeal

33. "Goodbye to all that," by Jonah Goldberg. National Review Online, September 23, 2005.

of state participation in charitable endeavours is a cruel and unrighteous proposition. It is simply conformity in social order to the conditions God has established and called us to enforce in His law. This is the God who loved His people so much that He sent His Son to die for their sins to bring His people to repentance and give them eternal life with Him. What Christian would argue that this God's propositions for the ordering of society are less gracious and charitable than His provision for eternal redemption? What Christian wants to argue that this God's principles for ordering society are morally inferior to those advocated by the adherents of another religion? We have nothing to apologise for as Christians for advancing God's law, including His teaching about the jurisdictional boundaries for the legitimate function of the state, the church and the family.

What we need to be doing, then, is taking up the challenge ourselves for the family and the church to take back the territory stolen from us by Canada's Secular Humanist civil government. That is really what we are doing when we tell the government to keep its hands off the definition of marriage. But we need to do this intentionally and comprehensively.[34] We need to see this skirmish, as important as it is, over the definition of marriage as but one part of a bigger picture; and we have to become committed to this bigger picture, committing ourselves

34. This may finally happen in England. The controversy over the Labour government's attempts to force all adoption agencies to allow homosexual couples to adopt children generated threats from Roman Catholic adoption agencies that they would have to shut their doors. Britain's pro-homosexual state-ists used the same rhetoric they use in Canada to argue against exemptions to such a law for Catholic agencies, marginalizing the contribution of Christians to the public square and government policy. In response, the Catholic church has indicated its intent to launch a major campaign to defend its role in public life ("Catholic Church plans fight to defend role in public life," by Jonathan Petre. The Daily Telegraph, January 31, 2007). It will be important to see how effectively Christians argue for the importance of their contribution to political theory and public policy, and whether they appreciate their unique and morally superior vision or feel the need to find some non-existent common ground with the totalitarian Secularists who rule the country as of the writing of this book.

to reinvigorating Canadian society comprehensively with the liberty ethic of Christianity, including an abiding commitment to a Christian-based sphere sovereignty.

Men need to be men again, and women need to be women. Men need to be husbands and fathers and women need to be wives and mothers. And we need to draw our line in the sand—a line well beyond where we are now—as we fight this war against the intrusion of the androgynous and sterile civil magistrate of Secular Humanism.

CHAPTER SIX

SHOULD CHRISTIANS BE IMPOSING THEIR VIEWS ON OTHERS?

A s discussed earlier, when "social conservatives" and Christians propose public policies and legislation that are based on principles and values that are not espoused by others, one of the leading arguments used against them by today's socio-political establishment is that nobody has the right to impose their values on others.

This attack invariably puts Christians on the defensive, and they respond with some version of, "We are not trying to impose our beliefs; we are just..."

Of course that is nonsense; it is just about as silly as are the premises behind the initial objection—that Christians have no right to impose their ideas by way of the democratic process that is accessible to others or that law and public policy do not by their very nature require the imposition of certain people's values on others.

Actually, the defence that Christians are not trying to impose our beliefs is not *complete* nonsense. Christians are not trying to impose their *beliefs* on others, they want to impose, or enforce, *behavioural norms* on our society. It is true that beliefs dictate what a person believes to be a behavioural norm, but it is not the beliefs that are being legislated, it is the behaviour. In fact, this distinction sets Christianity apart from just about all other worldviews including the systemically hypocritical Secular Humanism. Today, Secular Humanists condemn particularly social conservative Christians for wanting to impose their beliefs on others, yet it is Secular Humanism that is behind the gruesome and oppressive agenda to coerce people's consciences by requiring pro-life taxpayers to fund abortion. It is Secularism that supports the firing of Christian marriage commissioners who will not perform homosexual "marriage" ceremonies.[1] It is Secularism that opposes employment protection and the freedom of conscience for pro-life pharmacists, doctors and nurses who are not prepared to prescribe abortifacients or perform and refer for abortions.[2] And Secularism criminalizes speech critical of homosexuality and other Secular sacred cows. Christianity does not advocate group-think. Christianity does not require a declaration of war against people's consciences the way Secularism does.

At any rate, the fact is that unless society is 100 percent homogeneous philosophically (or abandons all of its legislation), then we will always face a situation in which

---

1. "Ziola resigns as Marriage Commissioner," by Lin Orosz. *Melville Advance*, January 19, 2005; "Some won't marry gay couples," by Michael Den Tandt and Shawna Richer. *The Globe And Mail*, February 3, 2005;"Gay-marriage foe takes fight to court," by Tom Brodbeck. *The Winnipeg Sun*, October 18, 2006; "To fulfill a marriage commissioner's duty," *The Globe and Mail,* July 20, 2005.
2. "Ontario Moving Ahead to Crush Pharmacists Conscience Rights." LifeSiteNews.com, September 14, 2005. "Accommodating conscience: Canadian nurses enjoy conscience rights ... to a point," by Greg J. Edwards. *BC Catholic*, October 14, 2002.

some people are being forced to comply with laws that limit their behaviour to a greater degree than does their own conscience—laws that require their compliance if they want to remain free from incarceration in that society.

People living in Canada are not unanimous in their views on whether or not female genital mutilation should be legal, or whether or not gun ownership should be legal. There is no unanimity on whether stealing (including extortionary taxation) or homosexuality, or capital punishment, or adultery, or murder (including abortion), or polygamy, or adult-child sex should be legal. We could keep adding to that list. All laws represent the imposition of a particular moral and philosophical—even theological—demand over all people, including those who do not agree with those laws. Christianity is not unique in this respect. The extended citation from Ted Byfield in Chapter Two effectively summarizes this point. It is part of the inherently dishonest nature of Secularism that has Secularists demonizing Christianity as uniquely oppressive because it supports the imposition of values on people who are not Christians.

Some people argue that a way around this is to allow for as many actions and choices to be legal as possible so as to allow for maximum liberty. At first this might sound like the common law, small government, laissez-faire approach of a bygone era when Christianity was the dominant cultural worldview. This, however, is not the case when it comes to the people advocating such a view today. The same Secular Humanists advancing this idea to, for example, sanction the new broader definition of marriage are among the most militant police-state advocates when it comes to curbing dissent, suppressing public expressions of Christianity. Most of these people also firmly position themselves on the left

149

of the political spectrum which advocates high taxation and an oppressive regulatory regime on the marketplace as well as restrictions on private property rights. These Secularists hate liberty. They only use the language of liberty to deceive and manipulate people into supporting their fight for sexual "liberty" alone.

The real issue is what choices should be free and what should be subject to criminal sanctions. To be sure, when this approach is driven by a Christian worldview, it results in a very limited scope of interest by the civil magistrate in the lives of citizens. Nevertheless, this Christian perspective does recognise a legitimate role for the civil government in areas where today's Secularists want complete freedom of choice, most particularly in terms of sexual behaviour. In other words, Secular Humanism demands (almost) absolute liberty from state regulations and prohibitions for sexual choices, while showing very little interest in a freedom agenda in any other areas of life, often in fact opposing liberty in other areas. Christianity, on the other hand, advocates a comprehensive vision of civil-social liberty, with the realm of sexual behaviour being one of the very few exceptions to this normative framework.

Those who argue that we should allow for as many actions and choices to be legal as possible so as to allow for maximum liberty believe that repealing the restriction on same-sex "marriage" makes the law more reflective of greater liberty by reducing restrictions and, therefore, the state's interference in this area.[3] As we have noted in the previous

3. They do not make the same argument to promote the repeal of other marriage laws such as those banning multiple spouses or marriages between close relatives because the state has not yet legalized polygamy or incest. These people are Secularists, so their god is the civil magistrate. Hence, their assessment of what is right and wrong depends on what is legal. If the civil government says certain behaviour is legal, then is it moral in their view. Because the Canadian government has not yet legalized polygamy, they do not see the logical inconsistency of their refusal to make the same arguments for polygamous marriage as they are making for same-sex "marriage." This has never been so obvious as in the comments

chapter, however, the trade-off is the elimination of this single expression of a state-imposed limit on access to marriage in exchange for a massive and comprehensive imposition of state-imposed regulations on marriage and family relations. The Secular humanist definition of "freedom" is found grossly wanting. And while it may benefit, in the short-term, the baser instincts of self-absorbed individuals who lack self-control, it is a definition that is at war with genuine civil-social liberty that maximizes the realm of ordered liberty for the largest proportion of civilized and responsible citizens.

Jennifer Morse addresses this perspective—"the 'leave-us-alone' ethos, as she puts it.

> The "leave us alone" ethos that lies behind the demand for the acceptance of all alternative families does not properly apply to the sphere of the family. Trying to equalize the outcomes for children requires that married couple families and childless people provide subsidies to those parents who dissolve their marriages, or who never form marriages. The state will be taxing the married to pay for the children of the unmarried. This is why the demand that the government be neutral among family forms is unreasonable.[4]

Posing possible solutions to the imaginary scenario of family breakdown that she painted (and which was cited in the previous chapter), Ms. Morse writes:

> A radical individualist might argue that the state should allow this couple to sink or swim on its own. If the

that former Liberal Justice Minister Irwin Cotler consistently made in response to people who were trying to make him realise the door he was opening for polygamous marriage by pushing through the redefinition of marriage to accommodate homosexuals.

4. "Deconstructing Marriage: Less Freedom; More Inequality," by Jennifer Roback Morse. *IMFC Review*, Fall/Winter 2005. Pp. 27.

man abandons her, tough luck for her and her child. If she kicks the man out, for good reason or no reason, tough luck for him. The social order simply can not afford to indulge people who can't get along with their closest and most intimate family members. If the state would get out of the family business, or charge people the full cost for the use of its services, fewer people would get into these contentious situations. People would be more careful in forming their intimate childbearing unions.

But our current ideological environment makes this position impossible, however much it might appeal to the radical individualist. The political pressures for the state to intervene on behalf of the unmarried mother are simply overwhelming. The welfare state is so entrenched that singling out unmarried mothers at this late date is not plausible. Given that reality, it is not realistic to expect the state to cease and desist from all the activities of the family court, no matter how intrusive or highly subsidized they may be.[5]

If the civil government did surrender all authority over the definition of marriage, that might be a truly libertarian approach to the issue. But that is not what Secular humanists have done. They have adopted a new definition and are imposing that on all Canadians, in some cases under threat of sanction. The fact that many self-professed libertarians have lent their support to the homosexual definition of marriage, despite its socialistic nature, demonstrates how superficial or intellectually convoluted modern libertarian thinking is. In fact, since the Christian definition of marriage is the most compatible definition with a civil-social order of maximum

5. Ibid.

liberty, libertarians should be strong advocates of real marriage. Needless to say, it is very unhelpful when Christians divide—and so neutralize—their forces, as when some advocate the notion that the civil government should absolve itself of any role in protecting a definition of marriage as though that were a strategic and biblically legitimate alternative.

Let us look at more examples in Canada's actual recent experience which demonstrate the freedom-hating nature of the homosexual "marriage" agenda. Public policy decisions work themselves out in real life and have real world consequences. In the context of Canada's current controversy over homosexual "marriage," we can see how provincial governments are ordering marriage commissioners to resign if they are not prepared to perform homosexual "marriages." One runs into the same problem with education. Public schools, being government-run schools, will teach the government-sanctioned morality as normative. The government will not provide different schools or classes for people who hold to different values. They could not afford to do so even if they wanted to.

This expectation has become a reality in British Columbia with the recent equality-hating decision in that province to allow two "married" homosexuals a unique status in vetting public school curricula. These homosexuals are so sure of their special position that one of the men, Peter Corren, has been quite transparent with his bigoted animosity towards Roman Catholicism.[6] These two homosexuals have also made it clear that they strongly oppose the parental right to keep their children out of classes that violate their values. "There

6. "Peter Corren dismissed the archbishop's statement, saying the church 'is continuing its homophobic diatribe against Canadian society. It's nothing more than we would expect from an organization that has victimized our society through history." "Gay school material a threat: Archbishop," by Janet Steffenhagen. *Vancouver Sun*, September 6, 2006.

was no point in us getting queer-positive information into the curriculum if it meant parents would be pulling their children out all the time," says Peter Corren.[7] Quite so—which exposes the monumental fraud of claims that religious liberty for Christians and homosexual "marriage" are mutually compatible public policies. Civil governments will advance either one or the other and even supposedly conservative-leaning governments like that of B.C. in 2006 are moving rapidly to extinguish the constitutional freedom of religion for Christians while they entrench special privileges for homosexual activists.

Other people have not been given such an influential position in B.C.'s curriculum development. Although he gave homosexual activists this special position of influence, British Columbia Premier, Gordon Campbell, dodged a rally of protesting parents, further disenfranchising these taxpayers and responsible citizens.[8] This is yet another example of homosexual sympathizers in government betraying voters and taxpayers by capitulating to the elitist agenda of homosexual activists who are demanding special privileges at the expense of Canada's old Christian-based commitment to genuine equality.

Parents who want their children taught differently, despite having to tax-fund these public schools, will have to choose a different education option for their children. This is oppression for people who used to be free—even if this change in the law grants liberty to people who were supposedly "oppressed." In fact, if one simply considered the demographic statistics regarding the number of Christians and the number of homosexuals in Canada, it would be clear that this move oppresses far more people than it liberates.

7. "Hooky touted for anti-gay parents: Trustee claims Education Ministry policy on opting out takes away 'freedom'," by Glenda Luymes. *The Province*, December 12, 2006.
8. "Campbell dodges protest." Letter by Stephen Gray. *The Province*, September 10, 2006.

Hence, the notion that changing the definition of marriage is a zero-cost measure that increases overall liberty in Canada is demonstrably false.

This observation about marriage commissioners and public school students also demonstrates that there is no honesty at all in the assertion that granting homosexual "marriage" rights is a harmless move for those who oppose the decision. We can see how much more serious this assault is on liberty in Canada when we think of the implications for those throughout the wedding industry (e.g. jewellers, florists and companies that sell and rent wedding gowns and tuxedos) who would have to look for new employment or violate their consciences due to the obligation to serve homosexual couples, not to mention Christian educators in the public school system, and many others whose lives will be impacted by this change in what the government wants to teach as normative reality and morality.

Regarding the trouble marriage commissioners are facing, Christians are arguing for freedom of religion and conscience on behalf of these commissioners. Politicians are saying that these commissioners are agents of the state and, therefore, have to comply with the parameters of what is deemed legal by the state. Frankly, logic is on the side of the politicians. If you carried the freedom of conscience and religion argument to its logical conclusion and allowed all commissioners and other agents of the state to exercise this liberty in every area where they felt the need to do so, you would have anarchy in the public service. What this points to is the fact that all religions or worldviews have implications for public life and the operation of the state. This is true for Christianity and for Secular Humanism. Christianity requires a certain definition and approach to marriage by the state, so when the law is changed in this respect, it represents an attack on

Christianity, a repression of Christianity, in that it revokes one aspect of Christianity as it is expressed in the public life of this nation. So, to re-assert the argument made earlier in this chapter, allowing homosexuals to "marry" does not introduce a value-neutral ethic into Canadian public life; it represents an overthrow of Christianity and its ethic at this point by Secular Humanism and its moral order.

Daniel Cere demonstrates the absurdity of treating the relationship between the civil law and marriage as value neutral and, therefore, a development that should not concern Christians in his 2005 report.[9] At one point in his report, Professor Cere observes that "laws do more than distribute rights, responsibilities, and punishments. Laws help to shape the public meanings of important institutions, including marriage and family."[10] Later he quotes William Eskridge, a Yale law professor and "a prominent architect of same-sex marriage strategy," arguing that "law cannot liberalize unless public opinion moves, but public attitudes can be influenced by changes in the law."[11]

Law in society is by nature an imposition. It will always involve an imposition on some people who do not agree with the law. As the Bible says, the law is for the lawless[12]. If we knew that no one in our society was going to murder or steal or assault others, we would not need to go to the trouble of establishing civil laws against those actions. The law exists to give us a knowable, predictable mechanism by which to incriminate and punish people who violate that law. When the objection appears about one group of people imposing their views on

9. "Future of Family Law: Law and the Marriage Crisis in North America," A Report from the Council on Family Law, Dan Cere, Principal Investigator. Institute for American Values, 2005.
10. Ibid., p. 10.
11. Ibid., p. 11.
12. I Timothy 1:9.

others, it generally relates to a particular legal obligation that the critics do not like—an obligation that they have decided to challenge. In other words, it is a fundamentally dishonest and intellectually incoherent accusation because it is not, in fact, an objection to all legislative impositions, just one with which those critics do not want to comply.

It is about time that Christians, especially those engaged in the political sphere, stopped being intimidated by this accusation regarding our desire to impose our beliefs on others. First of all, we need to be clear that Christianity does not support the imposition of *beliefs*. We also need to be clear that Christianity is not unique by way of its need to impose *behavioural norms*. Every competing worldview does the same thing. That is the nature of civil law. The only escape is anarchy, which is no escape at all.

Additionally, we need to teach others that, when compared to alternative political theories, particularly Secular Humanism, Christianity only seeks to impose a very limited number of behavioural norms by way of the civil magistrate. Christianity imposes many moral obligations on people, but only a very limited number of those obligations are to be enforced by the civil magistrate.

We need to be clear that Christianity does, indeed, advocate the imposition of some behavioural norms by the civil magistrate which a growing number of people in our culture think belong to areas of life where people should be free to make their own choices. This is most obvious in areas of sexuality, such that an increasingly guilt-ridden, sex-obsessed culture, which has been taught that sexual deviancy is victimless behaviour, wants to rid itself of legislation that criminalizes many of these deviant behaviours. [13]

Instead of acknowledging this fact, many Christians get tongue-tied and make fools of themselves, trying to claim that they are not imposing their behavioural norms on others. More intelligent critics actually read the Bible for themselves and show how this retreatist claim is false. By acting in this way, Christians undermine their own credibility and defeat themselves. This kind of cowardice or theological illiteracy is not the stuff of leadership, which is one reason that Christians are not taken seriously in Canada today.

It would be far better instead for us to acknowledge that law imposes, then start making the point that this is also the case for the Secular Humanist public policy agenda. At the moment, we are allowing Secularists to get away with cultivating the image that their ideology is far less imposing, when, in fact, the very opposite is true.

13. Christians need to clearly and forthrightly make the point that the Christian position advances the security of women over against the misogynist nature of Secular Humanism. Calling Secularism misogynist is not to imply that Secularists intentionally hate women; rather it is to say that their ideology treats women as though they were hated. U.S. columnist Mona Charen recently reviewed the book "Unprotected," written by Dr. Miriam Grossman, a psychiatrist at the student health service at UCLA. "She believes," wrote Ms. Charen, "that casual, promiscuous sex is tough on many women. They are hard-wired to bond with those they have sex with (the hormone oxytocin is implicated), and she sees countless female students reporting stress, eating disorders and even depression for reasons they cannot understand. After all, the world sells them on the notion that sex is pure recreation, that the 'hook-up' culture is natural and even empowering to women, and that love and sex are two completely different things." ["Unprotected," By Mona Charen. January 5, 2007. http://www.townhall.com/columnists/MonaCharen/2007/01/05/unprotected.] Secular Humanists are freed to reject Dr. Grossman's findings; it would be just another example of Secularism's growing hostility to science. The casual sex mentality brutalizes many women and when there are no laws against perverse sexual behaviour, these women have no recourse for the harm caused them. Civil law should not be the recourse in every case, but it does not follow by logic that no sexual behaviour should be criminalized. Cf. "Casual sex is a con: women just aren't like men." *The Times*, January 14, 2007, http://www.timesonline.co.uk/article/0,,2092-2545852,00.html; The Thrill of the Chaste: Finding Fulfillment While Keeping Your Clothes On, by Dawn Eden. W Publishing Group/Thomas Nelson. December 2006.

The Christian response should be: "Would you rather be subject to the Judaeo-Christian/biblical law-order or the impositions of Secular Humanism—or Islam, or Buddhism, or Hinduism, for that matter, or any one of a number of other options?"

"Law-order" is a vital concept in Christian political theory

That rebuttal introduces a new concept into this discussion: that of a law-order. Today, everyone talks about laws. When is the last time you heard anyone talking about law, singular, or a law-order? Have you ever heard any such discussion? Unlikely. We hear a lot about laws, particularly in the political realm, because apparently the primary responsibility of politicians is debating and passing laws. This is a devastating situation because without a law-order—an underlying philosophical base and intellectually coherent framework for legislation, there is no way to ensure that individual laws fit logically with each other, or to ensure an internal consistency in a society's criminal code. Laws are dealt with in isolation from each other (or only in relation to those few laws identified as immediately related). Much new legislation is introduced to solve specific, isolated problems, playing to particular competing interests. It is therefore anti-equality with politicians and judges showing little, if any, interest in maintaining an intellectually coherent and logically cohesive foundational law-order for governing Canada.

Of course, this situation should come as no surprise to Christians. The concept of a law-order—an underlying rational framework—only makes sense within an absolutist worldview such as Christianity. There is no philosophical context within relativism for the concept of a law order, which is why the relativism-based Secular Humanism that drives current Canadian public policy is so anarchic and convoluted. What is surprising, or at least disappointing, is how few Christians understand what has happened to Canadian public policy in terms of the abandonment of a belief in a law order.

As history and Christian theology indicate, anarchy is the fertile breeding ground for tyranny, and we are observing today a militant campaign for the entrenchment of tyranny and oppression in Canada. To give but three examples: We have no property rights; the government imposes heavy censorship on consumer access to news and other media; and tax dollars are used to fund political parties. Added to that, the freedoms of religion and conscience are being openly challenged. The intolerance and hatred that Secular Humanism affirms against Christians is palpable, not least by way of legislation and precedent-setting court and human rights tribunal decisions that effectively criminalize simple expressions of disagreement based on the Christian moral code.

If Christians do not understand the underlying reasons for this assault, if they are unable to distinguish between the working-out of Secular Humanism in civil life (including the legislative function) vs. the outworking of Christianity, they are going to expend their energy trying to combat the problem by tinkering inside a system that flows directly out of Secular Humanist philosophical assumptions and therefore a system designed to bring victory to Secular Humanism. This is a recipe for failure. If Christians are unprepared to challenge the philosophical foundations and rebuild Christian-based structures—legal, political, etc.—then all they are doing is targeting symptoms rather than launching all-out combat against the source of the attack on Christianity and our Canadian culture.

And Christians must understand that Secularism is so extreme that it even denies the ability of Christians (or others of "faith") to practice law. Remember the comment by David Rudenstine, the dean of Cardozo Law School at Yeshiva University cited in Chapter 1: "Faith challenges the underpinnings of legal education. Faith is a willingness to accept belief in things for which we have no evidence, or which runs counter to evidence we have. Faith does not tolerate opposing views, does not acknowledge inconvenient facts. Law schools stand in fundamental opposition to this."

Christians have to understand that Secular Humanism is not morally neutral. Christians have to understand that there is no such thing as a morally or philosophically or theologically neutral worldview or religion. Christians have to understand that biblical Christianity articulates the foundational principles for a legitimate, and therefore just, political structure, including a law-order. Christians have to be committed to doing the work necessary to re-discovering what these principles are, and learning how to apply them in the real world of Canada in the 21st century. Christians have to expect victory, and act accordingly. Christians have to be visionary, long-term thinkers; not short-term, knee-jerk, haphazard political actors.

Let us bring this discussion of a law-order back to the question of who should be imposing principles—not beliefs—by way of legislating behavioural norms, on others.

Christianity for a number of years now has been caricatured as an oppressive, legalistic religion that stifles individual liberty. Christians have brought much of this caricature on themselves. We saw many abuses against individual liberty during the "Medieval" era due to gross violations of the biblical parameters for the jurisdictions of the church and the state, with much confusion between the roles of both institutions. More recently, the legalism of "Fundamentalism" has understandably alienated many from the church. On the contrary, as we have discussed, and will explore further here, although God's truth and moral order provide for many impositions on our consciences, the biblical revelation suggests that only a very, very small body of law and impositions should be governed by the state.

On the other hand, Secular Humanists, having placed their faith in the civil government, and by extension, the civil law which the civil government administers, are fanatical legalists. And legalism, as the testimony of history and the Bible reveal, is the foundation for the most ruthless police states and tyrannical regimes. Conservative Jewish columnist Dennis Prager puts it succinctly: "Generally speaking, the Left and the Secularists venerate, if not worship, law. They put their faith in law—both national and international. Law is the supreme good. For most on the Left, 'Is it legal?' is usually the question that determines whether an action is right or wrong. ... [W]hy is the Left so enamored of law?... Laws are the Left's vehicles to earthly salvation."[14]

The biblical law-order governs all of life, and has implications for the state, for the church, for the family and for individuals in their personal relationship with God. These are complementary governmental bodies that all have essential roles to play in a robust social order. Hence, not all law and moral imposition has to originate with the civil magistrate.[15] In keeping with this framework, we find that the biblical law order provides for a very minimal role for the state. Or, to put it another way:

14. "The Left thinks legally, the Right thinks morally," by Dennis Prager. Townhall, September 21, 2004.
15. Marcus Tullius Cicero had the right idea centuries ago when he observed: "The more laws, the less justice." This could be the motto for 21st century Canada.

in the economy of God, very few sins are to be treated as crimes. As someone else has observed, Christianity has its 10 Commandments; humanism has its 10,000.

Regretfully, due to indifference or theological illiteracy, a large majority of today's western Christians have adopted many of humanism's commandments, finding convoluted ways to reconcile them with Christian morality. Invariably, they do this by observing that the law reflects a Christian moral position, but they do not evaluate the law in the context of the biblical law-order to determine whether the state has a rightful role in enforcing that position. As a result of this stance—along with the fact that Christians wanting to add (or preserve) impositions that very vocal opponents want lifted (usually related to sexual choices)—Christians contribute significantly to the impression that they represent a very oppressive and regressive religion or worldview.

If Christians were offering Canada a decidedly Christian view of government, then people would see a vision for government that saw the civil magistrate withdrawing its oppressive, expensive and divisive influence and control from a huge spectrum of areas over which it currently interferes. At the same time, it would reassert its right to impose sanctions over some areas, in particular, the whole area of sexual behaviour. Due to the addictive passion of perversion, many Canadians may be no longer willing to accept the trade-off of a more vibrant, profitable, competitive, laissez-faire economic framework at the expense of criminalizing a number of sexual choices. The fact remains, however, that a Christian law order provides for a much less intrusive civil magistrate than exists under today's Secular Humanist tyranny. Therefore, notwithstanding the initial frustrations that some people may experience over restrictions on their libertine behaviour, this Christian socio-

163

political model would provide for a much more profitable, less divisive, more free, just and equal society—such that a large majority of people would come quickly to support it, if only for self-interest and the benefits that accrue to them.

In their public comments, Christians must point out explicitly that Secularists do not promote genuine liberty; that Christianity is the only political alternative that offers a vision of comprehensive liberty. Christians need to explain that the licentiousness, lewdness and libertinism that Secularism advocates is not genuine liberty; that it is a narrow, self-serving agenda. Christians need to be able to show how, although the Secularist sex agenda may at first sound like a philosophy of liberty, it is part of an ideology that opposes fundamental principles of economic and political liberty as well freedom of speech, conscience and religion. If this is the case, how can the Secularist sex agenda be an agenda of true liberty? It cannot be. Such a notion is completely inconsistent and, therefore, irrational. Most Canadians presented with this evidence in an open manner would arrive at this conclusion on their own. Hence, the rhetorical trickery that Secularists use to hide their agenda, even stealing the Christian language of liberty and equity to paper over their true nature.

We have already seen a relatively healthy example of this Christian civil-social model in the Christian common law tradition of Western Civilization that ushered in and preserved 800-1000 years of *Pax Britannica*[16]. Canada shared in this

16. Cf. "It was Canada and New Zealand and South Africa, Australia, all these were standing by the side of the old Mother, and it was no longer England, or Britain, but it was that entity called the British Empire, that family, so difficult to understand, that preserved our common Christian civilization. ... the Pax Britannica means the Peace of Britain and the development of a people, the development of resources, order regulated under the law, and the administration of justice by the people themselves." An Address by Right Honourable The Viscount Bennett of Mickleham, Surrey, and of Calgary and Hopewell, Canada, P.C., K.C., LL.D., D.C.L. to a Joint Meeting of The Empire Club of Canada and The Canadian Club.

common-law tradition, and we saw the same benefits as other countries in terms of individual liberty, private property rights, limited, decentralised government, the priority of education, the development of hospitals, the care given to the poor, and principles of just jurisprudence such as equality before the law, the right to a speedy trial, being treated as innocent until proven guilty and the right to face your accusers.

Many of these dynamics still exist today (although in greatly weakened form), as do many laws that flow from a Christian law order such as the criminalization of rape, assault, murder, theft, slander and kidnapping. Most Canadians support these Christian values even if not passionately or in an intellectually coherent manner. Only the smallest minority of Canadians are self-conscious Secular Humanists. Unfortunately, many of them hold key positions of leadership and influence in society, and they know how to manipulate the levers of power and how to intimidate others to build the support necessary to make changes in law and public policy.

Leadership needed

All that is really needed for victory by Christians in Canada's culture war is what the United States has experienced in President George W. Bush: leadership – bold and courageous leadership. What Canada needs is a leader who is not afraid to speak openly about his faith and the implications of Christian faith in public life and social relations; a leader who has a comprehensive message of optimism and hope, promoting liberty, integrity and dignity, while also being unafraid to speak about the things he opposes and would even criminalize.

The Empire Club of Canada Speeches 1942-1943 (Toronto, Canada: The Empire Club of Canada, 1943) pp. 120-138. October 13, 1942

With Conservative leader Stephen Harper, Canada is once again experiencing genuine leadership. It does not go as far as is necessary to satisfy those whose concerns revolve around the so-called social conservative label, but on a number of issues where he believes strongly in something, where his government made promises during the election campaign, and where he does not think a firm position will undermine future electoral prospects, Mr. Harper is demonstrating leadership, and the difference between his approach to leadership and that of the dithering, equivocating anti-leadership of Liberal Prime Minister Paul Martin is palpable.

Ted Byfield makes this point in a column on Mr. Harper's positioning over the Israeli-Hezbollah war in Lebanon[17].

When Prime Minister Stephen Harper came out strongly on the Israeli and American side of the Lebanon controversy earlier this month, political commentators were largely in agreement about it. He had taken "a political gamble," one warned, while another spoke of the "risk" he was taking. What he was gambling with, they agreed, was liberal Canada's self-appointed role of peacekeeper and "honest broker" between militant nations, the role bestowed upon it by the Pearson government back in the 1960s and cherished by Canadians, so it has been supposed, ever since. In supporting Israel, Harper was not only rejecting this ostensibly sacrosanct Canadian model, he was also backing the much-assailed policies of George Bush. ...

As these charges were rained upon him by the liberal media, Canadians awaited the equivocating

17. "Ottawa takes a stand—for a change," by Ted Byfield. WorldNetDaily, July 22, 2006. http://www.worldnetdaily.com/news/article.asp?ARTICLE_ID=51181.

response so familiar from 13 years of Liberal rule. Instead, Harper came back with something so novel in a Canadian prime minister as to startle the nation: 'Harper Unwilling to Budge,' declared one front-page headline. 'Harper stands firm,' said another.

But the reaction was equally extraordinary. Congratulatory letters streamed into the newspapers. At long last Canada was standing for something, showing that we might actually have some national convictions (apart from an unflagging dedication to the rights of sodomists and abortionists).

Ted Byfield is not the only one noticing Stephen Harper's consistency in leadership as a marked deviation from the two Prime Ministers who preceded him. Kevin Libin, publisher of the *Western Standard*, also commented on it in relation to Mr. Harper's handling of the Israeli-Hezbollah conflict.

In the newsrooms of Toronto, [a Prime Minister with principles] is going to take some getting used to. They're still recovering from the fallout that followed their attack on the prime minister's defence of Israel in the Lebanese conflict. Or rather, the lack of fallout. When Stephen Harper said Israel had a right to defend herself, and called her response "measured," it made sense to most of us. ... But in the mainstream media, any conflict involving Israel is never so clear-cut. ... *Globe and Mail* columnist John Ibbitson warned that Harper had abandoned a long-standing policy of "Canadian even-handedness" in the region. The PM's comments were "stronger than prudence would have suggested." And since, following his statements, a family of eight Canadians were killed in the crossfire. He was surely regretting them.

... The next day's headline? "Harper refuses to budge." Say what? A leader who won't flip-flop on his foreign policy overnight? Even after media criticism? And after some civilians were accidentally killed? Sheesh. What's this guy on? Principles or something? Ibbitson was incensed at being ignored. Mr. Harper, he cautioned, you're making a serious "political gamble." Your remarks were "out of proportion." This would, he vowed, haunt Harper come election time. He wasn't alone. CBC political correspondent Keith Boag urged Harper to "reconsider" his position. ...

Harper had, the Globe assured us, ignited a "Canadian controversy." But what passes for controversy in newsrooms isn't necessarily as contentious on Main Street. Sure enough, days later, a CanWest/Ipsos-Reid poll proved that: a strong majority of Canadians—64%— believe Israel's response to Hezbollah was justified. ...[18]

Mr. Martin was known for being unable to make a single decisive decision. He seemed terrified of receiving any criticism for his decisions so he did not make any. The only exception, as Mr. Byfield notes, was his unflagging dedication to homosexuality and abortion. Mr. Harper, on the other hand, is taking firm decisions, with positions that the popular wisdom has identified as dangerous—choice in childcare, strengthening the military, smiling at U.S. President George Bush, declaring war on the Ottawa Press Gallery—yet with very little fall-out. Post-election ratings have demonstrated

18. "Uncommon Sense: Why reporters cannot stand a PM with principles," by Kevin Libin. *Western Standard*, August 14, 2006.

growing support for the Conservatives, support that puts them in majority government territory should another election be called. This kind of support does not come from mass conversion to conservative values, it comes from the appreciation that ordinary people have for genuine leadership, a dynamic that is very little understood these days, even by Christian conservatives. Christian conservatives need to learn from this experience and learn how to exploit this rediscovered support for conservative political leadership in Canada as they attempt to determine the right way to frame their "love-hate" relationship with a government that has a mixed track record in terms of adopting the public policy priorities advanced by Christian conservatives.

What many ideologues and idealists—across the entire philosophical spectrum—involved in politics and leadership do not realize is that they are weird; they are not normal. Their interest in philosophical precision and intellectual purity is not typical. Hence leadership and influence can be exercised without converting people to one's own beliefs and other dynamics must be used to attract support for whatever campaign you are working on. Political leaders need to understand better what motivates ordinary people. This provides direction in terms of what is necessary to appeal to enough people to gain the necessary support to be given a position of influence. It also provides insight into what kind of changes a person in leadership can get away with making without risking his ongoing position of influence. It is this latter area that should most interest Christian conservatives in the current cultural climate. A conservative politician, for example, is not going to win an election by campaigning on banning abortion and no-fault divorce. But does that necessarily mean that he will pay a political price if he tinkers with the law in these areas once he is in a position of political leadership? The answer is, "not likely." But most politicians do not appreciate this point, so most of them refuse to exercise the full scope of moral leadership that is possible and which God and their own consciences expect of them and which this nation requires of them.

The large majority of Canadians—and most people in free societies—are happy to live their own lives in their own communities without engaging in the bigger issues of life. They do not know what ideological Secularists believe, or why. They do not know what Christianity teaches, or why. And the large majority of them would conform their lives with little objection to whatever legal framework was put in place by their government to deal with abortion, environmental regulations, homosexuality, gambling, privacy regulations, pedophilia, securities regulations, drug use or marriage, as long as they were confident that they were living in a generally free and equitable society in which they could pursue their own dreams and ideals free from unwanted interference by people who would do them harm. Activists may be able to stir up short-term emotion, but most people just move on with their lives.

Because of the influence Secularists exert today, they can be very intimidating, if Christians do not know what they are about. But Christians should know what they are about, and we should know how effectively to combat the ignorance, bigotry and hostility of Secularists. It is the responsibility of Christians to prepare themselves in this fashion. This brings us to two concluding points, but let us introduce them by coming back to that earlier question:

"Would you rather be subject to the Judaeo-Christian/biblical law-order or the impositions of Secular Humanism—or Islam, or Buddhism, or Hinduism, or any one of a number of other religions?"

Canadians want equality and predictability before the law

In fact, although Secularists are completely preoccupied with the idea of imposition, most Canadians are not. They are much more down-to-earth than these ivory-tower ideologues. In any case, as we have noted earlier, the question is not *imposition vs. no imposition*, it is *whose imposition*—the imposition of one religion, worldview or philosophy of life over against the imposition of another. The large majority of "ordinary Canadians" understand this, at least implicitly. It is only ideological Secularists, consumed by their own convoluted irrationality and euphemistic imaginations, who may try to argue this point.

Christians should speak over the heads of Secularists to ordinary Canadians and not get caught up in the Secularist paradigm of imposition. What most Canadians are concerned about in terms of governance and law is equality and predictability, not imposition. Fleshing out this perspective on governance provides further opportunities to expose the tyrannical and oppressive nature of Secularism, over against the liberty found through the Christian civil-social model.

Equality before the law, or equality under the law, is the idea that all people will be treated equally if they are brought before the law under charges of having broken it.

"Equality before the law" is not a synonym of the phrase: "the repeal of laws against sodomy." You can look in any dictionary and you will not find those two phrases identified as synonyms for each other—notwithstanding the fascinating way in which homosexual activists quickly captured the terminology of "equality before the law" as the mantra for their political agenda. In fact, the concept of equality before the law has nothing to do with the particular content of the law; what actions should be against the law, and what should be legal. The concept of equality before the law simply says that if something is illegal—burglary, for example—then, if you are charged with violating that law, justice will be blind as it deals with you—i.e. you will be treated equally whether you are a man or a woman, black, white, yellow or red, or from Alberta or Nova Scotia. (This is not at all the concept of "equality" marketed by former Canadian Justice Minister Irwin Cotler or anybody in Canada's modern political establishment. It is categorically not the principle of equality as defined in subsection 2 of section 15 of the *Canadian Charter of Rights and Freedoms*. As we will discuss later, this concept of group equality, and the related idea of equality of outcome, flow out of the police state of Secularism.)

But there is another component to the correct definition of "equality before the law" that needs to be discussed. In fact, it is the most important component, without which the whole principle collapses. This component of the biblical/Western/ historic Canadian definition of equality before the law reflects the historic context that brought about the establishment of the principle. Hark back to the days of the *Magna Carta* in Britain and the conflict between King John and the British barons. The problem of inequality—that the principle of equality before the law was established through the *Magna Carta* to remedy—was the refusal of the king to be subject to the law of the land; essentially to remedy the problem of inequality between the king and his subjects, inequality between the governor and the governed. It reflects the voluntary social contract by which those who govern agree to subject themselves to the same law that is binding on all the citizens in that society.[19]

More recently, one of the many American leaders to uphold this principle was Justice Louis Brandeis, a judge on the United States Supreme Court in the early 1900s (and the first Jewish member of the U.S. Supreme Court). He said, "At the foundation of our civil liberties lies the principle that denies to government officials an exceptional position before the law and which subjects them to the same rules of conduct that are commands to the citizen."[20]

Under the guidance of the Secular extremist Liberal Prime Ministers Jean Chrétien and Paul Martin, Canada has almost completed the transition from a free and democratic society to a "banana republic." These two fanatics spat on the Canadian Constitution at every opportunity, as they ruled arbitrarily, and exploited every power lever to consolidate their power, reward friends and hide questionable and corrupt economic decisions. We have seen extensive disregard for Canada's Constitution in recent years by governors in every branch of government, by both politicians and judges—and government-protected bureaucrats.

When the governors no longer submit themselves to the same law imposed on the people, we have tyranny, not

19. It is voluntary because civil magistrates have the power of the sword at their disposal so they can always abandon their commitment to equality if they so choose. We notice throughout the world how difficult—impossible—it is outside of Christianity to establish a political order in which the governors willingly subordinate themselves to the principle of equality and refuse to use their positions for their own gain. Even many professing Christians fail this test of character. This is one of numerous examples which demonstrate the fact that political reform is impossible outside of a more fundamental cultural and spiritual reform. They must take place hand-in-glove.
20. Burdeau v. McDowell, 1921, http://quotes.liberty-tree.ca/quote/louis_brandeis_quote_8f2c. Cf. Olmstead v. U.S. (1928).

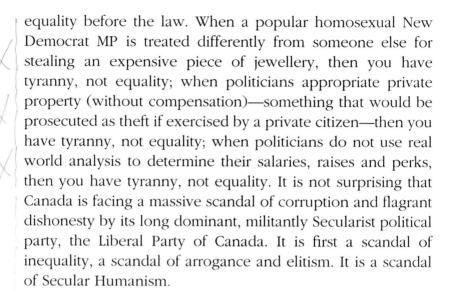

equality before the law. When a popular homosexual New Democrat MP is treated differently from someone else for stealing an expensive piece of jewellery, then you have tyranny, not equality; when politicians appropriate private property (without compensation)—something that would be prosecuted as theft if exercised by a private citizen—then you have tyranny, not equality; when politicians do not use real world analysis to determine their salaries, raises and perks, then you have tyranny, not equality. It is not surprising that Canada is facing a massive scandal of corruption and flagrant dishonesty by its long dominant, militantly Secularist political party, the Liberal Party of Canada. It is first a scandal of inequality, a scandal of arrogance and elitism. It is a scandal of Secular Humanism.

Secular Humanism, as we have already outlined, works itself out in society in demonstrably different ways from Christianity; and one of those ways is its hostility to equality. Christianity elevated the principle of "equality before the law" in the socio-political order. As the influence of Secular Humanism rises, that commitment to equality disappears, and in its place we increasingly face arrogant, self-righteous, pretentious, self-serving governors intent on building their own power-bases and empires in order to impose their own narrow, oppressive and socially destabilizing agendas on an entire people.

Another example will help to illustrate the all-encompassing impact of the "thugocractic" ideology of Secularism. Most of us would like to see our governments achieve success against organized crime. Hopefully, though, most Canadians still reject the ethic of "the end justifies the means." One of the unacceptable means to combat organized crime that has become popular in recent years here in Canada (and in the United States) goes by the name of "proceeds of crime" legislation. The federal Liberal government, under the guidance of the radical Secularist Justice Minister Irwin Cotler, introduced legislation that would increase the government's power to confiscate people's property if it is believed to have been purchased from the proceeds of organized crime.[21]

This legislation reverses the onus of proof in terms of allegations of criminality where alleged proceeds of crime are found. In other words, if the government seeks permission from the courts to confiscate a person's property, the law requires the accused person to prove that his possessions are not from the proceeds of crime—rather than requiring the government to prove that they are—if he wants to stop the police forces from taking his property. Mr. Cotler's bill specifically applies a reverse onus of proof in proceeds of crime involving offenders convicted of a criminal organization offence or certain offences under the *Controlled Drugs and Substances Act*.

In other words, this kind of legislation treats a person as guilty of an offence until he proves himself innocent. It is a disturbing abandonment of another fundamental Christian principle of justice – "innocent until proven guilty." The *National Post* issued a warning about the legislation, but the Conservative Party of Canada actually supported it.[22] The *National Post* warned:

> … Asset forfeiture laws present enormous potential for abuse unless they are carefully drafted. In the United States, it took the passage of the comprehensive

---

21. This legislation, Bill C-53, was introduced in Parliament on May 30, 2005.
22. The Conservative Party's March 2005 Policy Declaration proposed: "An amendment to the Criminal Code to reverse the burden of proof, so that the members of a criminal organization (and not the Crown) will have to prove at the time of seizure that the goods were not acquired through criminal acts."

Civil Asset Forfeiture Reform Act (CAFRA) in 2000 to curb overreaching by law enforcement agencies. Before CAFRA, authorities were able to seize property—something as small as a sofa, or as large as a mansion—from suspected drug dealers before they had the opportunity to defend themselves at trial. … Mr. Cotler should be equally careful about how the proceeds from seized assets are dispersed. Under any new legislation, proceeds should go to the general treasury—not, under any circumstances, to the law enforcement agencies directly involved in policing or prosecution. To do otherwise, clearly, would create unhealthy incentives for officers to be overly vigorous in pursuing arrests and convictions.[23]

The principle of equality before the law is not a stand-alone principle. It is part of a comprehensive, Christian vision of justice that includes other principles, such as innocent until proven guilty, the right to face your accusers, the need for at least two witnesses to be found guilty of a crime and the right to a speedy trial. Regardless of where else they may be found, all these principles are taught in the Bible and, historically, for the West, were derived from a Christian worldview. It is not surprising, therefore, that Secularism has declared war on every one of these principles as Secularists seek to accomplish a comprehensive transformation of Canadian society from a liberty-oriented civilization to a deadly police state. And proceeds of crime legislation is just one example of the way this vision reaches into every area of life and our social order.

Supporters of proceeds of crime legislation have argued that the principle of innocence until proven guilty does not need

23. "The perils of easy forfeiture." Editorial. *National Post*, March 11, 2005.

to apply because the people whose property the government wants to expropriate are not being charged with a crime. Therefore the civil standard of proof (balance of probabilities), not the criminal standard (beyond a reasonable doubt), applies. That argument may be technically legitimate, but it reflects a complete rejection of the spirit and intent of the law. Private property rights are an essential component of the vision of Christian liberty, a vision which places a very high threshold on any attempts (including by civil governments) to take this property from its private owners. Hiding behind an argument about "not needing to apply the criminal standard of proof" demonstrates an attitude of utter condescension by arrogant, elitists against the citizens of the nation who are supposed to feel secure in the just and equal application of the law.

The dishonesty in the assertion that the law is acceptable because it does not require a criminal standard of proof is transparent when it comes to Mr. Cotler's legislation. His Liberal government bill had a provision to fine a person in lieu of confiscating his property, and another provision allowing for the imprisonment of that person if he does not pay the fine. In other words, Mr. Cotler's proceeds of crime law allowed the government to imprison someone without the person even being charged with a crime, let alone being found guilty. This is a ruthless example of the police state agenda of Canada's Secularists and an ominous sign of the diabolical tyranny we can expect if Secularism's extremist adherents win the culture war against Christianity for control of this country's political system.

Of course, these tyrants hide their arrogance and ruthlessness behind language with which we are comfortable, even behind the rhetoric of equality itself, but by equality, they do not mean individual equality before the law. They are die-hard Secularists, socialists, state-ists. When they refer to "equality," they mean group equality, not individual equality, and, as part of that concept, they mean equality of outcome, not equality of opportunity. And, of course, equality of outcome means the use of state-imposed mechanisms, such as affirmative action and quotas, to achieve the outcome they desire. In other words, they market discrimination, bigotry and racism under the guise of equality, redefining the term so that it means to them the very opposite of what it means to those who still operate, intentionally or otherwise, within the context of a Christian-based vocabulary.

As indicated earlier, the large majority of Canadians are happy to live their own lives in their own communities without engaging in the bigger issues of life. For the most part, they would be able to adjust their lives quite easily to fit within the variations of law and politics that fall within the realm of current political debate. They have accommodated themselves to an increasingly pro-criminal "justice" system and to a stagnant economy in which they are muddling along without seeing any real rise in disposable income for years. So, it is not far-fetched to imagine most of them being willing to accommodate a legislative environment which includes laws against perverse sexual behaviour that most of them do not engage in anyway—and, even if they did, they could probably continue to do so (although perhaps less frequently) below the radar of the civil magistrate—especially if there was a genuine trade-off in which the new legislative environment also radically freed up the marketplace to allow for far superior possibilities for wealth creation and productivity.[24]

24. PQ leader Andre Boisclair does not agree. In comments about concerns he had regarding a possible Stephen Harper led government, he has said: "Are we saying that the price for settling the problem of fiscal imbalance is to say the right to abortion no longer exists? Are we saying the price for fixing the fiscal imbalance is rescinding the Kyoto accord? Quebecers do not want to pay this price." ("Quebec isn't Tory country, Boisclair says: Views

What free individuals really want is fairness and justice. Primarily, this means knowing that they will be treated the same way as everyone else before the law. This also means living in an environment that is legally predictable. This means everything from not having police (or child and family services agents) knocking down your door or trying to push their way into your home without a warrant, to living in a society that is governed by laws that are elementary enough to be understood. Convoluted legislation undermines the principle of predictability. A tax code that is so complicated that you need a professional to complete it for you undermines the principle of predictability. Living under the burden of so many regulations that you probably break one or more every day without even realising you are doing so betrays a society that has completely abandoned any serious commitment to the principle of predictability.

This growth of a socialist, centralist, interventionist state in Canada has taken place alongside—and as a result of—the erosion of Christianity in this country. Ronald Reagan put it poignantly: "Sir Winston Churchill once said you can have 10,000 regulations and still not have respect for the law. We might start with the Ten Commandments. If we lived by the Golden Rule, there would be no need for other laws."[25]

The oppressive, tyrannical regime under which we live today in Canada is the "gift" of Secular Humanism, as this militantly anti-Christian ideology forces its way into place as the new official religion of Canada. Christians governing Christianly would re-establish the principles of equality before the law

on abortion, Kyoto differ; Charest says he is 'helping Quebecers,' but not taking sides on Harper vs. Martin," by Philip Authier. *Montreal Gazette*, December 22, 2005.) He may be right; then again he may be wrong. This thesis has not yet been tested. But Harper's Conservatives did win the last election with a breakthrough in Quebec.

25. Patriot Post, Vol. 07 No. 03, January 15, 2007.

and predictability into the public policy of Canada in the context of a coherent, understandable law-order. At the same time, they would ban some behaviour that is currently legal. In light of the liberating effect of the overall program, it is very likely that a return to a Christian approach to law and governance would be greatly welcomed by the large majority in Canadian society—even if it takes some time of bold articulation to communicate the Christian vision to our fellow-citizens. Christianity's agenda of individual liberty and equality before the law would likely win wide support in Canada, even today.

How long do we have to wait for Christian reformation?

This brings us to our second, and final, concluding point. We cannot wrap up this discussion without addressing the question of whether the kind of revival of Christian leadership in civil government outlined here is likely to be realised, and how long it would take to see it become a reality. Many Christians are hoping to implement a "social conservative" political agenda regardless of whether or not Canada sees a growth in personal conversions to Christianity. They hope that both dynamics take place alongside each other, but they do not seem to think that conversions and the growth of the church are *necessary* to successful political action.

The fact is that the kind of biblical Christian reformation outlined above will *only* be realised when a sufficient number of Canadian Christians become possessed of the faith and vision necessary to see it realised. Many Christians today are talking about a revival of prayer, repentance, enthusiasm and emotion in churches and Christian meetings. By various criteria, a number of Christian leaders around Canada are claiming that we are in the midst of a revival. Perhaps. But these criteria are not sufficient.

How will we know when Christians possess the faith and vision necessary to regain ground in Canada's public square? Because we shall see results, and we shall see intersecting results on several fronts. We will see Christians committed to addressing the sin and wickedness of Secular Humanism and its consequences in a bold and forthright manner. We shall see Christians courageous and intelligent enough to set the terms of debate instead of trying to fight within the parameters set, and on the terms dictated, by their opponents. We shall also see a renewed commitment by Christians to participate in public life in every area, recognising their obligation to be involved and recognising the fact that their participation is necessary to replace the oppression, ignorance and inhumanity that dominates each profession today with a commitment to justice, genuine equality, charity, human dignity and mercy. Genuine Christians do not participate in public life to gain power, they participate to serve.

At the same time that we see all these things taking place, we shall also—simultaneously—see a renewed movement of Christian conversions. This may actually have to be the first dynamic we see as evidence of a new and vibrant Christian faith and vision. Christianity is a "bottom-up" religion, not "top-down." But it is not bottom-up as understood within a humanistic, materialistic or exclusively political framework; it is bottom-up in that it depends for its success on the transformation of individuals' beliefs, priorities and values through conversion.

At a theoretical level, as discussed, a Christian public policy and legislative civil-social model could well be widely accepted by a non-Christian populace because of the attractiveness of the ethic of liberty that it implements; but in reality, such a model requires a substantial level of homogeneity of belief in the populace in order to achieve long-term and sustained success. The spiritual realm is real, and the dynamics of sin and temptation are real.

One of the reasons why today's Secularists find such an affinity in the general population for their perverse agenda, even if that support is only skin-deep and very fickle, is that they appeal to the broad-based recognition by people of their personal failure to live up to their own ideals; they appeal to people's recognition that they bend the law here and fudge there—nobody is a rigid law-keeper. Hence, when activists make arguments about the need to relax the law in one area or another, when they frame their arguments with cunning and drive them home through repetition, it is very easy for them to convince enough people to support their agenda to influence polling and manipulate governments. These Canadians, however, could with similar ease be convinced in another direction as well, but only people who understand their own worldview can offer others a convincing and compelling vision of service and liberty.

The faith and vision of genuine, theologically literate Christians is greater than that possessed by the adherents of any and every other religion—because Christianity exclusively is true, and Christianity is the only religion which directs its adherents to a God who is alive—and the omnipotent (all-powerful) Sovereign of creation. When we start to live an active Christian faith and vision, Christians will see conversions, and those conversions will translate into greater Christian involvement in every area of life, including areas of influence such as civil government, law, education and journalism. As a result, we shall also see greater Christian influence and leadership in the crafting of law and public policy, and the re-Christianisation of Canada.

The Kingdom of God is spiritual. The correct meaning of this is that the Kingdom of God embraces both the physical and the immaterial realms. It has implications for both spheres, and it needs to be worked out by God's people in both jurisdictions. There is spiritual work to do such as repentance, prayer and evangelism, and there is material work to do such as discipleship and training into full-orbed Christian living that has implications for both private and public life in Canada, including the way in which the civil magistrate governs this country. Let's get busy.

CONCLUSION

I n Canada today, Christianity is at war with Secular Humanism. This protracted conflict has been going on for several decades and has been fought on numerous fronts. Secular humanists are fighting for total victory, and they have a clear picture of the goal they are pursuing. This has not been the case for most Christians. This is the main reason why Secular Humanists have won most of the skirmishes in this battle.

Secular Humanism is socialistic in nature. It advances the proposition that society can only function when the state has total control over all of life. Secularists abhor the idea that the family and the church should exercise governmental responsibilities over their own distinct spheres of life. Secular Humanism also works, intentionally or otherwise, against the nurture and development of self-government. The advancement of Secularism has taken place—logically—

alongside the erosion of freedom of conscience, freedom of religion, freedom of speech and the freedom of the press. Secular Humanism lacks philosophical categories to make sense of individual liberty.

Authentic Christianity, on the other hand, offers men a philosophy of liberty. It is primarily a message of spiritual liberty, liberty found in redemption and eternal life through Christ. But Christianity is also much more than that. Christianity is a comprehensive worldview, and it is a worldview established on a dynamic principle of liberty that weaves its way through every aspect of a social order set up under the direction of biblical principles. A Christian social order is much more appealing to people than the tyrannical and oppressive alternatives advocated by other religions and worldviews, especially the ruthless police-state model being advanced and nurtured today by Secular Humanists.

So, why do not more Canadians express support for this Christian worldview? Because this is not the worldview advanced by most Christians today. We Christians need to re-discover this worldview, adopt it for ourselves, learn to love it, and learn to communicate it passionately and attractively, if we want others to join us with their own enthusiasm for this worldview and the liberty it offers to all law-abiding citizens.

When Christians limit their opposition to Secularism to particular issues that happen to strike them as particularly offensive for one reason or another, instead of confronting Secularism as a worldview, we almost guarantee defeat at the hands of our enemies. When we address the symptoms of the problem, instead of trying to pull up the root, we show that we do not really understand the nature of the battle we are waging; and certainly any victory we might gain is likely to be short-lived.

Charles Colson has provided an inspiring summary of the significance of the Christian ethic of liberty in terms of the values and policies Christians have advanced in history. It is worth reprinting here in its entirety.[1]

> It was one of the most poignant pictures to come out of Iraq: a smiling young woman, holding up a finger stained with purple ink—proof that she had just voted in the first election of her life. It was evidence, as well, that America had gone to Iraq, not to conquer, but to set people free.
>
> The idea that freedom is the state in which God intends us to live is found in the Bible. The Indian apologist Vishal Mangalwadi makes this clear in his teachings. In a tape on how the Bible influenced the second millennium, Mangalwadi says the prototypical model is the Exodus. This was the first time that people were delivered from slavery and bondage, and a record made of it. This, Mangalwadi says, "is what changed the whole course of Western civilization—the notion that God was bringing us freedom."
>
> The belief that humans deserve to live in freedom is what motivated Americans to fight for their own freedom from the British. It motivated us to fight Nazi Germany and the Japanese during World War II, and against communism during the Cold War. And it's what motivates us today to bring freedom to parts

1. "Soldiering Justly: Fighting Freedom's Battles," Charles Colson. BreakPoint, May 30, 2005.

of the world that have never known it—Afghanistan and Iraq. This fight for freedom has the additional advantage of striking a blow against terrorism. Once people are given freedom, they will fight to protect their freedom against terrorists who are determined to take it away.

This willingness to sacrifice on behalf of our neighbors is why serving in the military is considered such a high calling for Christians—and part of what makes just wars just. Thomas Aquinas in the *Summa Theologica* puts his discussion of just war in his chapter on charity—the love of God and neighbor. Aquinas applauded those who wielded the sword in protection of the community. Reformer John Calvin agreed. He called the soldier an "agent of God's love" and called soldiering justly a "God-like act." Why? Because "restraining evil out of love for neighbor" is an imitation of God's restraining evil out of love for His creatures. And as Darrell Cole, a professor at William & Mary, argued in the journal *First Things*, the failure to fight a just war may be a failure to love. Fighting just wars, he wrote, "is something Christians ought to do out of love for God and neighbor."

A world where all Christians refused to fight just wars wouldn't be peaceful, and it certainly wouldn't be just. It would be a world where evil reigned unchecked by justice, and where the strong would be free to prey on the weak. The mass graves in Iraq—graves dug during Saddam Hussein's reign of terror—are grim evidence of this truth. While the polls show that many Americans are becoming tired with the war in Iraq, our soldiers who are stationed there are not. They know they are doing a good and noble thing.

One way you might celebrate Memorial Day today is by watching a film being premiered tonight on HBO, *Unknown Soldier: Searching for a Father.* I was not able to attend the preview, but I'm told it is deeply moving and will fill you with gratitude for those who have laid down their lives to set us free. And it will cause you, I hope, as well, to pray for those who are still fighting for freedom around the world today.

Christians who are fighting for genuine liberty—including socio-economic and political liberty—have nothing for which to apologise. Such Christians should be—must be—proud of their commitment to advancing the application of the law of God as the laws and public policy framework for their nation. Canadians will thank them for their commitment, while history turns Secular Humanism into a byword. Christians who love liberty and Christians who love their fellow man should be passionate about wanting to introduce the one to the other. We have work to do.

ABOUT THE AUTHOR

 Timothy Bloedow has worked as a researcher, speech writer and media coordinator for two Members of Parliament in Canada's federal government. He is a writer and a real estate investor. He worked as a researcher and lobbyist for Campaign Life Coalition. Mr. Bloedow has run for office as a member of the Christian Heritage Party of Canada. He co-founded and published *The Ottawa Times*, a monthly newspaper, in the early 1990s.

Mr. Bloedow has a Bachelor of Theology from Tyndale Bible College (then Ontario Bible College). He is married to Lynette and has two children, Ulyn and Daniel. He is motivated by a desire to explain and advance the comprehensive claims of Christ over every area of life.

www.christiangovernment.ca

Printed in the United States
88765LV00003B/4-99/A